Feeling Normal Again

A Post-Pandemic Guide to Emotional Health

By Stephen J. Kristof

Feeling Normal Again; A Post Pandemic Guide to Emotional Health
© 2021, Stephen J. Kristof

All rights reserved. No part of this publication may be reproduced, distributed, or transmitted in any form or by any means, including photocopying, recording, or other electronic or mechanical methods, without the prior written permission of the author or publisher, except in the case of brief quotations embodied in a book review and certain other noncommercial uses permitted by copyright law.

First Edition: December 2021
ISBN-13: 9798774947980
Copyright Registered, U.S. Library of Congress
Registration: TX 9-059-168

Some names and identifying details have been changed to protect the privacy of individuals. The case scenario couple of "Terry and Trevor" is fictional. Their names and situation are completely fictitious; any resemblance to actual persons, living or dead, is purely coincidental.

Cover Design and Photography by Stephen J. Kristof, © 2019

Disclaimer:
This book is sold with the understanding that neither the author nor the publisher is engaged in rendering any professional advice, or mental health or physical health services to the intended reader. This publication and the ideas presented in it are intended for entertainment and information purposes only, and are not meant to diagnose or treat any mental or physical health disorder or disease. This publication is not intended to be interpreted or used as a substitute for consultation with or care by a licensed mental health practitioner or physician. The author is not a medical or mental health practitioner. Please consult with a competent, professional, licensed physician or mental healthcare specialist regarding any of the tools or suggestions made in this book.
Best efforts were used to ensure that the information in this publication is accurate, however the author and publisher disclaim any warranty as to the accuracy, completeness, currency or contents of the publication. Contact information contained in this publication with respect to suicide hotlines, was accurate at the time of publication, but no warranty is implied for accuracy at any later date.
Exercise and physical fitness are discussed at points in this publication; the publisher and the author strongly recommend that you consult with a physician before beginning any exercise program, fitness or sport. If you engage in any exercise, fitness or sport, you agree that you do so at your own risk, are voluntarily participating in these activities, assume all risk of injury to yourself, and agree to release and discharge the publisher and the author from any and all claims or causes of action, known or unknown, arising out of the contents of this book.

The author and publisher of this publication disclaim any liability arising from contract, negligence, or any other cause of action, to any party, for the publication contents or any consequences arising from its use. The use of this book implies your acceptance of this disclaimer.

For my Parents,

For my Mom, Irene. Your abundant love, strong faith and continuous encouragement have shaped my life. I am truly blessed for these gifts and thank you for making our family your priority.

For my Dad, John. You will always be remembered for your love of our family, for your patience and for how you made visitors to our home feel welcome and valued. I am very fortunate to have had you in my life.

"MY LIFE HASN'T FELT NORMAL SINCE COVID."

You are not alone! Covid-19 and its variants have left wounds and scars that most of us are feeling, although we're not fully aware of exactly where they are or how deeply they are affecting us.

This is a crucial book for the times. It helps define how the pandemic has affected and changed you, and provides dozens of effective healing strategies to help you feel normal again.

PRAISE

"The author provides strategies to imply in your day-to-day life in hopes that you heal from the emotional and social damage caused. While we are fully aware of the effects of what happened and are still dealing with the situation, Kristof points out ways for us to take control of what is lost.

I mainly found this book helpful because it didn't just go over the everyday things we are all uniformly affected by. It even covers things like recharging our faith in gaining hope. The literature is written well and is targeted at anyone who wishes to deal with the post-pandemic. I recommend it to everyone since we all – in some shape or form - had to deal with COVID-19."

Jeyran Main
Editor-in-Chief, Review Tales Magazine

"Stephen Kristof's new book addresses not only how the pandemic has affected our emotional, social, political and spiritual health, but that of our country and beyond. His book outlines the challenges we've faced and provides coping tools. It will not only resonate with (local) readers, but with the world over. Feeling Normal Again is about healing and hope."

Veronique Mandal
Host, Scribes and Songsters (TV series)

"COVID is still around (I have it here as I type) but the pandemic does seem to be winding down. It's not gone but it's time to start rebuilding our lives, our relationships, our jobs and our mental health...This little book is a pretty good guide to how to heal from 2 years of pandemic hell. For each potential impact to our lives, it is discussed in detail. Impacts such as sleep problems, anxiety, COVID PTSD and so much more.

Chapter 5 is your personal emotional toolbox and includes tools such as treat your body well, focus on the positive, and renew friendships and start new ones. Copies of this book should be in every library. It's time we get back to normal."

Kathleen Garber
SMS Non-Fiction Book Reviews

CONTENTS:

INTRODUCTION: Some Initial Thoughts............	vii
CHAPTER 1: How Did We Get Here?.....................	1
CHAPTER 2: Where are We Now?.........................	25
CHAPTER 3: The Media's Role.............................	35
CHAPTER 4: How Are You Feeling?......................	43
Impact #1 – Sleep Problems..	45
Impact #2 – Malaise...	48
Impact #3 – Worry and Anxiety......................................	51
Impact #4 – COVID PTSD...	54
Impact #5 – Boredom with What was Previously Interesting..	61
Impact #6 – Lack of Motivation and Constant State of Fatigue......................................	68
Impact #7 – Fear of Doing Ordinary Things.................	70
Impact #8 – Social Anxiety..	77
Impact #9 – Broken Relationships.................................	79
CHAPTER 5: Personal Emotional Toolboxes.........	83
Toolbox #1: Pay Attention to Your Feelings....................	84
Toolbox #2: Treat Your Body Well.....................................	87

Toolbox #3: Reduce Screen Time and Avoid
        Certain Media.. 93
Toolbox #4: Focus on the Positive....................................... 100
Toolbox #5: Take Control of Your Anxiety...................... 111
Toolbox #6: Renew Friendships and Start
        New Ones.. 120
Toolbox #7: Reintroduce Structure and Routine........... 132
Toolbox #8: Get Out and Get Moving............................. 140
Toolbox #9: Keep Up Appearances................................... 144
Toolbox #10: Repair Your Relationships......................... 149

CHAPTER 6: Healing From Loss............................ 159

CHAPTER 7: Resilience... 167

**CHAPTER 8: "Is Our World Really that
        Fragile?"**.. 185

CHAPTER 9: Retiring During Covid..................... 193

CHAPTER 10: Believe in God................................. 209

CHAPTER 11: Believe in Good............................... 225

End Notes.. 232
About the Author.. 236

Introduction
Some Initial Thoughts

Have you changed since Covid-19 made its ugly appearance and impacted everything about how our world works? It's highly unlikely that you somehow evaded its impact; most of us have changed in significant ways that are directly attributable to the pandemic, whether we realize it or not.

I wrote the original introduction to this book back in November 2021, but saw the need to revisit it. I didn't fathom back then, that so long afterward, we would continue to be plagued by emotional, social, physical and even political distress from the pandemic and its lasting effects! This addendum to my original introduction is an important reminder that the wounds are still fresh and if we do not intervene in their healing, the resulting emotional scars will continue to cause discomfort.

We hear others say it all of the time. We sense that something is just not right. We're not really sure what it is, but life doesn't feel 'normal' the way it did before the pandemic began. It's easier to blame it on Covid and walk away without solutions than it is to recognize that it is WE who have changed and that we need to make adjustments.

That's not to say that the things and routines that used to make life feel normal haven't changed; they certainly have! Things like supply chain shortages, restricted travel, employer expectations, political upheaval and healthcare squeezes have all contributed to life feeling abnormal when contrasted to life before Covid. However, those factors merely scratch the surface of explaining why so many of us feel so 'off' and why life doesn't seem normal as it once did.

I wrote this book to help you understand the specific ways in which the pandemic may have changed you and to provide tools that will restore the feeling of normalcy that we all crave.

Life is a precious gift and we cannot allow Covid or any other scourge to stand in the way of living that gift fully and with gratitude!

The rest of this introduction and the book itself is the original text. It is even more relevant today than it was in first printing.

(Original Introduction)

At some point in May 2020, a few months after everything had pretty much ground to a halt in North America and elsewhere around the globe due to the Covid-19 pandemic *(scientifically identified as the SARS-CoV-2 virus)*, someone in the media carelessly used the term *The New Normal*. From that point forward, the term caught on and not just with the news media. People began tossing the expression around in everyday conversation; conversation that, for the most part, was occurring remotely between people.

It was so eerie to have our lives upended seemingly at once and to have the entire world come to an abrupt halt without much warning. I was concerned when I first heard a news reporter utter the words, "the new normal," because there was an ominous sound to it. I cringed with fear that such a mindset could gain traction to quickly have universal acceptance. I was even argumentative with friends and family who dared to speak those words; I don't think they understood why I was so vehemently opposed to the term or its darker meaning.

I was concerned for a lot of reasons; chief among them being the impact such language could potentially have on our collective consciousness of living in a world that we believe will be forever altered in largely negative ways. I worried that this "new normal" mindset might lead to a loss of many progressive liberties that had taken so long to attain, that it could stoke fear about never being able to climb out of the harmful fallout from the pandemic and that it could lead people to focus on the relatively few ways that we are different rather than the overwhelming majority of ways that we are the same.

I was also very worried that the pandemic would lead to fear and distrust of each other, stoking what was already a growing wildfire of division in our society. We can now see that this has happened. Worrying if the person waiting next to us in line at the grocery store or walking past us on the sidewalk could infect us with Covid made us suspicious of one another; unfortunately, this distrust still lingers. As much as wearing masks in public was a crucial element of preventing spread of the disease, it also provided a constant visual reminder that other people could be dangerous. Even from the early stages of the virus, masks also became a political football that pushed us further away from each other.

Moreover, I feared that if people accepted that the new and very strange ways of going about life would become the new normal, society would lose hope.

What didn't make sense to me was how people could fall into a trap so willingly, that they, themselves, began spreading the doom and gloom to anyone who would listen. To actually consider that *this is it*; life as we have always known it is now over and has been replaced with this weak and, frankly, horrific version moving forward. What an awful nightmare. What a terrifying movie. What's worse – it was, or at least seemed to be, real.

It's not like the world hadn't previously suffered from pandemics; think about the Spanish Flu, the Hong Kong Flu, (H1N1) or SARS, just to name a few from the last 3 or 4 generations. Of course, countless other pandemics and deadly outbreaks over the course of human history made their own impacts, but this time around we had some advantages that the world did not previously have. Medical science and technology has never been as advanced as it is in modern times; vaccines, biologic therapies, advanced ventilators, and other medicines and treatments created a new battlefield upon which to fight this enemy.

Regardless, humanity was hit hard by this scourge and continues to feel the pain. With over 5 million deaths reported globally as of November 2021 it was a shocking reality. The gloom seems to have stuck with so many people in so many different places. With Christmas approaching, this menacing coronavirus was still a thing. Nearing two years of Covid-19, it was easy for doubt and fatalistic thoughts to pop into our heads. "Maybe this IS the new normal. Maybe this thing will just keep mutating and will never go away. I guess we just have to accept that masks, shutdowns, social distancing, messed-up supply chains, limited travel, loss of vacations and messed-up economies are all part of what life looks like from now till the end of days..."

Winter made an early appearance in many states and provinces in 2021 and with it, new concerns arose from medical experts, due to people returning to gathering in indoor environments. They were also worried about the general population's lack of immunity from the seasonal flu, since we skipped an entire year of it as a result of wearing masks and other restrictions. By U.S. Thanksgiving, rates of infection and severity of disease continued to differ significantly from jurisdiction to jurisdiction, as did their continued adoption of preventative measures. Several U.S. states had removed most restrictions and people appeared to go about their business in normal ways, but some of those states that opened up the earliest were also experiencing worrisome upticks in infection and hospitalization. California, for example, was just one state that in November 2021, was preparing for a fourth wave in the coming winter months. At that same time, Michigan was leading the nation and hospitals there were once again becoming overly burdened.

Meanwhile, the nation watched as major indoor sporting events opened to tens of thousands of crowded fans cheering their teams - with hardly a mask to be seen. The juxtaposed images and messages were confusing. Further concern began to percolate when it was revealed that some jurisdictions that had the highest and earliest adoption of full vaccination among residents, were starting to see an increase in infections and hospitalizations among fully vaccinated people, indicating that immunity was waning earlier than had been hoped. That concern turned to panic when, on U.S. Thanksgiving weekend, a new and highly contagious variant, dubbed "Omicron," began to circulate.

It was beginning to look pretty bleak; the world was exhausted and we all needed a break. What became obvious was that, those feelings of depression, lack of motivation and angst appeared to hang over our lives. Even though it's clear that the end of the pandemic is within eyeshot, for many, those negative thoughts and feelings persist.

This book examines the pandemic within the context of shared concerns, confusion, social divisiveness, political upheaval and numerous personal emotional wounds; the collateral damage of the Covid-19 pandemic. More importantly, it provides concrete strategies to address and overcome these ills. Ultimately, the goal is to feel normal again; to worry less, to enjoy life more and to be happy. There's one other thing I hope my readers get out of this book and it's just that...**Hope**.

Chapter 1
How Did We Get Here?

Do you remember feeling "normal"? All jokes aside *(perhaps you're a card carrying member of the "I Was Never Normal to Begin With Club"...)*, this really *is* a serious question. This book focuses on strategies to help us heal emotionally as we enter or move toward the post-pandemic phase. After experiencing the physical, emotional, social, cultural, economic and political fallout from the Covid-19 pandemic, many people feel that they are trying to climb out of a deep pit. Unfortunately, just getting out of that pit has not necessarily provided the sense of normality that we so desperately need.

The feeling that something is not right in our lives, in our communities or even in the world can gnaw at our subconscious, working its way through to our conscious thoughts, making it difficult to complete the simple tasks in life, let alone the complex ones. This is a common outcome of any personal trauma and can linger well after the cause of the trauma has resolved. In the case of this pandemic, it was both personal and global; its impact struck the entire world. The lingering angst has worked its way through our collective consciousness.

Recognition of the fact that we are not yet feeling normal has been echoed at the highest levels. On November 6, 2021, President Biden stated during a press briefing, *"...this is a confusing time...the world has never been here before."* Biden continued, saying, *"I have one focus...how do we get you to the *point where we take pressure off you so you can begin to get back to the degree of normality and we move to a different place?"*[i]

The shock of the pandemic and the ensuing lock-downs felt overwhelming at first. Throughout most of our lifetimes, we never experienced anything that so suddenly and completely stopped the world. At the same time, we began questioning everything; our health and that of our loved ones, our jobs and even our freedom. As the pandemic went on for a year, along with all of its nasty baggage, we became frustrated and angry. When it continued well into the second year, we became depressed and many of us lost a chunk of our hope.

We may be slowly pulling out of the pandemic, but its impact continues. When a huge swath of the globe's population continues to feel that something is just not right, that collective consciousness can have devastating effects on the way we live our lives, raise our families, do our jobs, elect governments (where such freedom exists) and how we allow ourselves to be manipulated by false messages that are designed to manipulate society. On a personal level, this lingering feeling – the loss of normalcy – leads stealthily to the inability to make decisions, lethargy, anxiety, depression and the loss of a sense of how one fits into one's own world.

So, how did we get here? Here we go...Happy New Year! Well, really not at all. Just days into 2020, the New York Times published an article by reporter Sui-Lee Wee about an illness that was hospitalizing and killing people in Wuhan, China; a city that was unknown to most North Americans and therefore seemed like it was a million miles away. The article was a bit concerning, but since it was far from our own backyard, it was also easy to dismiss. The headline, "China Grapples With Mystery Pneumonia-Like Illness," turned out to be one of the most important – and prophetic - headlines of the year, foretelling of a virus that would turn our world upside down and bring life to a halt in ways that we could not fathom and had not experienced in generations.[ii]

Just two months later, it was becoming evident that this "Novel Coronavirus" was cause for serious concern. Most of us didn't want to think about it. However, we all had some level of recognition deep in our subconscious minds that this new virus and its impact could get very, very bad. By March 11, 2020, the World Health Organization (WHO) declared the outbreak to be a global pandemic. Just days after that, the Center for Disease Control (CDC) issued a no sail order to all US ports pertaining to cruise ships as it became clear that the massive vessels were breeding grounds for the new virus.

Still, many North American families and students were busy getting ready or had already departed for their spring break vacations, while other weren't so keen on going anywhere. Droves of would-be travelers cancelled their trips as the national mentality started to take-on a hunker-down approach. The brave ones *(or reckless, depending on your perspective)* kept their reservations and went away regardless. Depending on where they went, people who did choose to travel during the month of March returned home to a reality that was far different from when they left. Northern travelers who went to Florida to warm up, catch some rays and relax on the beach couldn't believe their eyes when, upon returning, found that their hometown grocery store had more empty shelves than food due to panic buying. Others who left just a few days later were too late. Many travelers found themselves temporarily stranded as airlines domestically and around the world began cancelling flights on a massive level.

The world was starting to shut down. Governments began examining the transmission rates and modeling, and came to the conclusion that they would quickly run out of hospital beds and ventilators if infection rates continued to climb. In response, lockdowns, stay-at-home orders and severe restrictions were enacted globally in both authoritarian and democratic regimes. In most jurisdictions, non-essential services, workplaces and public activities were shut down until further notice. For the most part, people understood why hitting the pause button was a difficult but necessary sacrifice for the local, national and global good. During this early stage of the pandemic, it was only a very small minority that made some noise about individual rights being trampled. As we now realize, that small minority would grow.

Admittedly, many people actually enjoyed the sense of calm that the pause button provided, giving them a chance to reflect on and reprioritize the most important things in their frenetic lives. For urban dwellers, the silence was such a rare and beautiful break. Initially, it seemed odd not to hear the constant din of factories, cars, construction, planes and trains. However, that silence eventually became deafening to many ears, as the lockdowns continued and we longed for things to return to normal. When life came to a standstill in mid-March, our collective hope and expectation was that this thing would burn itself out over the following few weeks to a month, and that soon after, life would return to normal. Generally speaking, most people didn't expect the restrictions to last much past Easter 2020, which was in mid-April.

Easter came and went, as did our shared patience for the ways in which the pandemic had restricted and changed our lives. It finally dawned on us that this was here to stay for a while. In fact, we started to wonder when, or *if*, our lives would ever return to normal.

"The New Normal" is a term that should never have been uttered about this pandemic. It's not a new term, though. Shortly after it began percolating through the media in early spring of 2020, CBS News pointed out that The New Normal was initially seen in print as early as 1918, following the end of World War I.[iii] The network observed that following every major catastrophe since then, people have focused on the idea that life will fundamentally change. It's no surprise the concept of a new normal comes up repeatedly during catastrophic times; we humans have a hard time adapting to change. The idea of a new normal is part of dealing with the insecurity surrounding change. Tragic events and milestone achievements, alike, can bring lasting change and different ways of living for individuals. On a societal level the same thing happens; whether it is a calamity like war or a pandemic – or – something positive like a new technological advancement, we start to wonder and worry about how it will change the comfortably familiar aspects of our lives in potentially good and bad ways.

 The September 11, 2001 World Trade Centre attack created a sense of panic not only in New York City, but around the globe. It didn't take very long for people to start speculating about how the tragedy would impact life everywhere and, potentially, permanently. I was at work when it happened. A good friend and coworker ran in to tell me what he had just heard. We fashioned a coat hanger and some scrap wire to create a makeshift antenna for a large television set in my area that had been used exclusively to show VHS training tapes and movies. Watching in horror as the buildings burned and crumbled, and listening to the correspondent's narrative speculating about international terrorism, I said, grimly, "This is going to change so much of our lives for a very long time. This could be very, very bad."

 Where were you when you first heard the news? The reverberation was felt so universally that, to this day, if one types, "Where were you..." into a Google search, the engine will complete the sentence, with "on 9/11," as the first and most popular search string for those three words. Searching the phrase, "Where were you on 9/11," generates roughly 489 million results. For Baby Boomer and older generations, a similarly popular question was, "Where were you when John F. Kennedy was shot?"

What's the point? We tend to judge the significance of events by their resonance with memory; in other words, the degree to which people continue to talk, write and think about events defines their importance. Over two and a half years after Covid hit the world, it's proving to be a hugely important event. Search Google once again, but this time try searching "Covid Timeline." That will generate about 1.5 BILLION results.

When something major happens in the world around us, we tend to bookmark it and treat it as a defining moment in our lives. We intrinsically understand that, the more significant the event, the more likely and more deeply our lives will change. And, frankly, most people are not very good at accepting or adapting to change, so whether or not we want to think about it, the thought hangs over our heads.

Sadly, a significant negative social paradigm resulted from 9/11. A new normal was born; it impacted everything in our world related to domestic and international security. Of course, air travel went from something that was rather pleasurable to becoming far more stressful, time consuming and difficult; it still is, compared to taking a flight pre-9/11.

Reaction to the attack also led to the war on terrorism including, of course, US-allied forces' feet on the ground in Afghanistan. It took 20 years for that "Enduring Freedom" initiative to formally end, with the US finally exiting the nation in September 2021. With a cost of over 8 billion US dollars and the lives of over 7,000 US troops and contractors, not to mention scores of other allied soldiers and shockingly, over 70,000 Afghani and Pakistani military and police personnel, troops ultimately left the region with little to show for these obscene monetary and heartbreaking human costs.[iv]

The angst that people experienced back in 2001 with respect to *that* new normal, proved to be foretelling when one looks at what occurred in Afghanistan and Iraq. However, it went well beyond that and changed many other aspects of our daily lives including the way we think. For one thing, we found that the national and local focus on safety, protection and security cameras became a systemic obsession. It permeated our thoughts and changed the way we perceived each other; some even began to view others with suspicion, particularly others whose cultures were markedly different from their own. In many instances, some viewed people of different cultures or ethnicities with abject suspicion and a prejudgment of guilt. Most worrisome, the new normal spawned by 9/11 included a systemically-experienced and deep personal insecurity. Our vision of the world as being a generally safe place and our faith in our fellow person as being generally well-intentioned was severely damaged.

Fast-forward to the Coronavirus pandemic and, once again, we faced another barrage of new normal worries and predictions. In early spring of 2020, the media grabbed the new normal phrase and wouldn't let go. People around the world were pelted with the phrase from news media and social media sources. "Experts" were already making predictions about when the pandemic would end along with even grimmer predictions about what the new normal would look like.

Some of the predictions were laughable and far-fetched, while others seemed rational and scary as hell. The worst ones, the frighteningly prophetic scenarios, often came in news headlines and during sensational interviews with bona fide experts and, sometimes, quacks that appeared to be credible. The fearsome predictions gained even more credence through reinforcement, as other news media, social media and even our loved ones, friends and neighbors repeated them in casual conversation.

However, the conversation from spring of 2020 through autumn of 2021 was, more often than not, anything but casual. In fact, sociologists and psychologists noted that after a year of being isolated from social friends and acquaintances, most people had somehow lost the art of conversation along the way. The conversational deficit was even worse for those who were working at home because of the pandemic. Without daily interaction with coworkers, many people began to feel at a loss for words when they found themselves, unexpectedly, in what were previously comfortable and non-threatening social situations.

From the early stages of the pandemic up to as much a year or longer, many people around the world simply stopped socializing on a physical basis. Many just didn't feel comfortable with the idea of being in the same enclosed room with others; after all, if we weren't able to work with others, attend school, meet with our doctor, go to church, sit down with our financial manager or even – so very sadly – attend a friend's funeral, then how on earth were we supposed to feel safe attending an indoor social gathering? Beyond that, in many jurisdictions, indoor social gatherings were banned or severely limited to immediate family plus one outsider who lived alone.

For many, "Socially Distanced" outdoor get-togethers with a limited number of friends or relatives as well as impromptu front-lawn gatherings with neighbors on widely spaced lawn chairs helped to fill the social void through the warm months of 2020 (during those times during when such gatherings were deemed legal). For those in temperate climates, when the weather became too cold to attend outdoor social gatherings comfortably, a new trend emerged. Do you recall the giddy novelty of attending a remote Zoom meeting with friends or relatives from the comfort of your own home? It was fun, at least at first, to raise a glass of wine and toast in unison with several people appearing in little boxes on our screens, but it was also very artificial and unusual...not to mention that the conversation was severely stilted and carried just a fraction of the substance when compared to the in-person variety.

Different regions of the world went through cycles of establishing, relaxing and re-establishing various social restrictions during the recurring "waves" of the pandemic. When lockdowns eventually ended and restrictions were loosened, people finally started braving the fun and exciting world of socializing with friends. But, for many, it didn't seem fun or exciting at all. As social scientists warned, many of us had actually lost the art of conversation. An evening out with friends, something we looked forward to so eagerly, turned out to be rather dull, monotonous and in some cases downright painful! It seemed that we had lost our collective interest in each other, and in any news beyond divisive politics and the fallout from the pandemic.

Living through a year and a half long pandemic can create much more chaos than, merely, a collective social ineptitude. Alarm bells rang as rates of depression in young people rose sharply through the pandemic. High rates of depression, anxiety, panic, lethargy and other mental health issues continued to persist even after the pandemic began to subside, and experts warned that the fallout would be as challenging to treat as the physical symptoms were at the pandemic's height.

Making matters worse, even as late as the fall of 2021, we heard dire warnings that the virus would continue to mutate forever, making masks, social distancing and shut-downs a never-ending cycle. The bad news and ominous predictions created a hunger for more of the same. It was both plausible and fearsome; the world would never shake this virus, it would continue to eat away at our population, just as water eventually erodes everything in its path.

Much like a depressing song's refrain, we kept hearing a discomforting chorus of voices. "Hope you enjoyed it while you had it; things will never get back to where they once were in terms of employment, travel, the economy and, in general, much of our hard-fought freedom. In-person workplaces will be a thing of the past for many, so you better make that temporary workspace in your home a permanent office. In-person socializing will never return, so you better get used to lifting that glass of vino with your friends over a Zoom meeting. Restaurants, in-person shopping, and attending professional sporting events and festivals are long-gone."

Being in the grips of the virus carried with it a huge emotional toll. Even though we may not have contracted the virus ourselves, many of us experienced the loss of a loved one or of an acquaintance, or were merely reminded of how menacing Covid was when we learned that a prominent individual or celebrity was fighting for their life in ICU or had just expired from it. By the summer of 2021, most people on this globe had been through a series of lock-downs, and many consecutive months of mask-wearing and social distancing. Four months later, as autumn arrived, it dawned on people that we had dealt with this thing for over a year and a half, and health experts were forecasting at that juncture that we might not be out of this mess until the spring of 2022 – a full two years...or longer.

The earlier threats about the new normal began to appear like more of a reality than a threat. After all, the world was a very different place than it had been almost two years prior and it became even more plausible that what we had known as "normal life," would never fully return. Our way of life and things that we had done without question previously had become distorted and sometimes carried an air of frustration, negativity and, ultimately, submission.

For example, once indoor dining was opened-up again, the opportunity to indulge in a romantic dinner with your special person or to meet with friends for dinner and drinks was, for many, fraught with worry and indecision. While a good chunk of the population seemed to have no qualms going about their lives without that worry or indecision, a considerably large proportion of society wasn't ready; they weren't so eager to live life so fully or quickly. It was frustrating for those in the *"not ready to do that yet"* camp to see the rest of the world seemingly getting back to normal, while they felt that they were nowhere near that point and honestly wondered if they would ever get there.

We either experienced directly or heard stories from friends – countless stories - of families being torn apart due to diametrically opposed factions that either wanted to or wouldn't be caught dead attending a wedding, traditional holiday celebration, funeral or reunion. You most likely experienced something of the sort in your own life. As 2021 dragged on, the decision to attend a social gathering of any sort became a nightmare for some, while others partied-on.

To make matters worse, it became clear that another divide was opening even wider; the chasm between the vaccinated and those who chose to avoid the Covid vaccine. While it was a personal decision in most free parts of the world *where a vaccine was available*, the reasons why the unvaccinated made their decision were troubling. Now, let me be clear about one thing here. Although this book is primarily about post-pandemic emotional HOPE, HEALING and RESTORATION, there are historical truths and realities that we must come to terms with before we can move on. The awfulness of the Covid pandemic was conflated with a rather recent phenomenon of politically-driven lies, half-truths, misinformation and outright disinformation that resulted in a state of affairs that was far worse than had we only wrestled with the pandemic itself. This is a very important concept that cannot and should not be ignored; especially within the context of the post-pandemic fallout. History has a way of repeating itself, but understanding why bad things happen and what made them worse can potentially reduce the chance that they happen again.

What exactly created such a thunderous anti-vaccination voice? After all, in 1954, in response to the devastating effects of polio, Dr. Jonas Salk's vaccine went into trials with over a million children in the US, Canada and Finland getting a jab of the miraculous preventative in a program that was considered a calculated risk. A year later the vaccine was deemed safe and effective, and became part of routine vaccinations in countries around the world. Despite initial hesitation, the Salk vaccine enjoyed tremendous public acceptance in the US and Canada even though it initially involved our youngest people. What was different between the 1955 acceptance mindset and that of 2021? Primarily, it was a respect for science that has eroded severely in recent years.[v]

One huge difference between 1955 and the present is that social media did not exist back then. Some aspects of social media are positive. It can legitimately claim some degree of positive influence for various regional and global achievements, such as helping to develop social momentum by supporting grass roots campaigns to gain increased freedom in authoritarian regimes. Similarly, social media has helped spread a growing awareness of the need to combat global climate change. Allowing individuals to express their beliefs, ideas and experiences to others on a scale not previously possible is, yet, another potentially positive upshot of social media.

Nevertheless, there are an awful lot of ideas being expressed through multiple social media channels and platforms that are filled with nothing more than fluff and ego. It's not too much of a stretch to consider that the majority of content carried through social media is essentially fluff and is driven by ego. There's nothing really wrong with that. It's called entertainment and, in some cases, can even be educational. However, there is a reason that, traditionally, this type of stuff would never make it into what used to be called the "mass media." Much of the content on blogs, viral tik-toks, popular tweets, etc., can't make it past the gatekeepers that are an essential part of professional broadcast, print and electronic media. Vetting for truth, verification from at least three credible sources, ensuring political balance, avoiding editorial subjectivity; these have long been the tenets of professional news media gatekeeping in legitimately free nations. The concept of gatekeepers and their value is part of the foundation of the news media; it is something that I learned was *untouchable* during my university days in communications and broadcast media, and I saw it applied routinely in my early career working for a major TV and radio network.

Admittedly, a media gatekeeper can be used improperly. Once a "professional" media outlet or, as in the case of modern-day media – a gigantic cross-media monster – uses the gatekeeping function as a means to manipulate content, then its role has been corrupted for the gain of power and money. As a means of maintaining objectivity in the words you're reading right now, I'll refrain from labeling any major TV network as being ultra-conservative or left-wing liberal, but suffice it to say that there are very loud and persuasive voices out there that have dishonored the tradition of free media by transforming gatekeeping into something that excludes valuable perspectives, balance and…are you ready for this…truth itself!

Following a particularly combative and divisive era in US politics, by 2020, the assault on truth reached new heights in ways and at depths not previously seen in modern times. Internal and external forces worked very hard to spread disinformation that was overtly intended to bolster political base and power. This was achieved through spin and transparent messages that erased negative realities, replaced truths with lies, introduced absurd terms like "alternative fact" and propagated outright falsehoods fashioned from nothing but thin air. Another shameless term, "fake news" was born and was used, ironically, to describe truthful news that these despicable architects wanted us to believe was false. So confusing, but it worked. HOOK, LINE AND SINKER! The hook was set with falsehoods, lines were cast to biased news outlets and un-vetted social media, and the message sunk in deeply with a faction of the public.

This social media that did not exist back in 1955 was a highly influential force in 2020 and is even more so today. So, what created the huge backlash against Covid vaccination? Disinformation, outright lies and heavy-handed scare tactics, to be frank. Politically biased news media, un-vetted social media streams and contextual targeted advertising fed a consistent torrent of junk science and dishonesty to a political base that eagerly gobbled it up. You see, one way of maintaining political power is to promote ideological concepts and constructs that resonate with the political base; apparently, whether or not they are true no longer matters. It's shameful but it is a reality of our times. Unfortunately, the divide that's resulted from all of this propaganda has had a devastating impact on the general concept of truth, social harmony, political fairness and, in the case of this book, the physical and emotional well-being of people.

Are the approved Covid vaccines completely, 100%, unequivocally safe in all respects for every single person? No, not for every single person who gets jabbed with one. But neither is any vaccine. Then again, the chance for adverse effects from approved Covid vaccines was and continues to be exceptionally minute compared to the far higher potential for getting very sick or dying among those who remain unvaccinated. As 2021 progressed, it became increasingly clear that the vast majority of serious cases of disease and death resulting from the virus were, not surprisingly, among the unvaccinated. At the same time, there were only extremely rare reports of significantly life-altering conditions linked to the vaccine.

In a sense of fraternal stewardship, vaccines protect everyone from a larger threat. Personal choice is a blessing in a truly free country, but we must remember that freedom comes with great responsibility to one another. That sentiment has somehow been lost amidst the very vocal, yet marginal antivaccine crowd. The flames of this particular fire were fanned by the aforementioned politically-generated lies and propaganda. The barrage of anti-vax lies effectively influenced tens of millions of Americans to avoid getting a jab for their own good and for the good of their fellow citizens.

Earlier, I had mentioned that some of the predictions of our "new normal" were so preposterous that they were laughable. Some of the anti-vax lies were and continue to be equally preposterous, though they seem believable enough to many.

Chances are, if you're reading this you don't follow conspiracy-driven social media and audaciously biased news outlets. As a result, you may not be familiar with the many "alternative reality" lies about Covid vaccines that have been circulated abundantly by these information channels from late 2020 and throughout 2021.

*The following points are presented in quotations
to underscore that they are not fact,
but were mistakenly quoted as fact.
Here are the more popular ones,
however absurd they may seem:*

- *"The vaccine contains microchips to track everyone and steal our freedom."*

- *"The vaccine actually causes the variants."*

- *"You will become infertile due to the vaccine."*

- *"Your body will become magnetic as a result of the vaccine."*

- *"The vaccine doesn't work; your own natural immunity is far better at fighting the disease."*

- *"The vaccine actually causes people to become sick with Covid."*

- *"Vaccinated people spread the virus far more than the unvaccinated."*

- *"The vaccine causes autism."*

- *"Being vaccinated puts you and your children at greater risk of contracting the disease."*

- *"The vaccine contains deadly toxins at deadly levels."*

- *"The vaccine is the mark of the beast, as foretold in the biblical Book of Revelations."*

- *"The downfall of humanity and the end of times will be a result of the Covid vaccination."*

True science easily debunked these lies, so why did so many people accept them as truth? The answer is simple and is one of the foundations of brainwashing. Reinforce the opposite of what someone knows to be true and eventually that same person will accept the lie as truth. That's correct. Repeat a lie enough times and it becomes truth. The process is no different from the basic one behind the propaganda machine that was created in Nazi Germany, reinforcing lies to generate anti-Semitic beliefs. While Hitler used Joseph Goebbels to plant lies and harvest hate, so, too, have some modern-day politicians done the same type of thing.

A politically important base on the far right was hungry for validation. By spreading lies about the vaccine and propagating them through the channels mentioned above, that base eagerly consumed the disinformation. Doing so encouraged that same base to distance itself further from the competing party. It also gave the impression that the other party was an enemy – a contemptible enemy – because they were trying to peddle poison to the masses. Some people refused to get vaccinated because they didn't want the other party – the newly elected party – to succeed or to be seen as successful; it's hard to believe but, true. How pathetic when you consider what was at stake!

Sadly, although this effort may have resulted in political gain, it also created collateral damage in three distinct ways. First, it drove an even bigger wedge into the U.S. political scene, further eroding democracy and threatening national safety. Second, it cost an untold number of lives by discouraging healthy people to stay healthy by getting what is truly a miracle vaccine. And, third, it further contributed to a collective and individual sense of gloom, uncertainty and anxiety by dividing a nation.

By analogy, it's sort of like telling people repeatedly, that the sky is purple until they actually believe it. When droves of others join in the Purple Sky Movement, the leaders fabricate dogma that unites them together with greater purpose and determination, like for instance, the belief that Purple Sky folks are the only true patriots, while the Blue Sky folks are the worst kind of traitors. Along comes a full solar eclipse; a rare marvel to witness. Welding filtered eyewear is made available in advance to all citizens, free of charge, from the federal government. Unfortunately, the Purple Sky people are somehow convinced through alternative fact peddlers, that looking directly at the sun is safe and healthy. The Blue Sky group promotes the use of the special eyewear for everyone's sake. However, the Purple Sky folks are manipulated to believe that the glasses will make them go blind. They continue to look directly at the sun, unprotected. However, they are confident in their decision because they know certain "truths"; they are patriots, they are in good company and the Blue Sky folks are trying to harm them.

Okay, it's quite a stretch, but deserves a few marks for creativity. But seriously, think about where peoples' emotions end-up through the above scenario. Leading up to the eclipse and afterward, people are left feeling exhausted, angry, divided, defeated and anxious as hell. However, a striking difference between this situation and the Covid one, is that in the story above, the people who refused to wear the eclipse eyewear did not pose a health threat to the ones who chose to protect themselves.

Back to the real-life situation; by November 2021, an increasing number of corporate entities, public organizations, transportation carriers and governments made good on their promise to exclude the unvaccinated. Several professional sports leagues and individual teams also required their athletes to get fully vaxxed, a decision that cost some reluctant star athletes several millions of contractual dollars. Many of the large venues that hosted those same teams also required fans to be vaccinated in order to attend games.

This collective effort to promote vaccination rates did just that. It came down to the old maxim, "Put your money where your mouth is." It's one thing to stick to deceptive conspiracy bunk about not being vaccinated which, for many, became intertwined with their personal ideologies. However, it's quite another thing to do so while facing the looming consequence of losing one's job, not being able to board a plane, being barred from a major event or enjoying countless other freedoms. Predictably, although millions acquiesced and got their shots, the uproar got even louder.

During the last three months of 2021, the world waited for the other shoe to drop. Of course, we had already seen that shoe drop over and over again, as health officials responded to ongoing pandemic waves with cyclic restrictions that, frankly, were becoming very old. Some real hope hovered over the horizon with things in some U.S. states and in certain parts of the world getting closer to the "normal" that we all remembered.

Stadiums started to fill with tens of thousands of unmasked fans cheering on their beloved team, select concert venues came to life once more with throngs of young people singing, cheering and dancing, and restaurants, many which were on their last financial legs, welcomed patrons for indoor dining. People picking-up curbside orders were in a small minority compared with the throngs of shoppers inside malls, stores and supermarkets. Various personal services returned to the menu of allowable non-essential business activities in many jurisdictions. Millions of people were returning to work at the office (while millions of others chose to retire or quit because they had time to contemplate a different sort of life).

From a cursory glance, everything appeared to be on-track and life was returning to normal. However, warnings came in the form of increasing numbers of cases and deaths in areas that supported full-on pre-pandemic living. Florida, Georgia and Texas opened their states fully for business before most others, despite criticism from experts in the health sector. In these states and others that dropped mandatory masking and other preventative measures, infection numbers rose. In early August 2021, while Florida was dealing with record Covid infection numbers, the state's governor characterized reporting on such statistics as fear mongering and media-fueled hysteria.[vi] The rhetoric didn't seem to help the situation; by the middle of October, 2021, Florida's Covid deaths were among the highest in the nation, as reported by the New York Times.[vii]

However, as the last few months of 2021 moved along, Florida's numbers precipitously dropped; by November 23, 2021, Florida had the 10th lowest per-capita number of deaths from Covid, and the second lowest per-capita new case count among all 50 states. That was good news for Florida and they weren't alone. It seemed that other states which had dreadful numbers just a few months prior, also appeared to have turned the corner. It certainly looked optimistic, but it was also confusing.

In the summer of 2021, states, provinces and nations with the highest vaccination rates, not surprisingly, had the lowest incidence of new cases of Covid and deaths occurring from the disease, while jurisdictions with the lowest rates of vaccination had embarrassingly high infection rates, hospitalizations and mortality. However, inexplicably, by late November 2021, the correlation between vaccination rates and infections became unclear, as some states with high vaccination rates experienced sudden spikes in infection and deaths, while some with very low vaccination rates were doing far better. One thing was clear, though; the contradictory numbers just added to the general confusion and uncertainty surrounding Covid.

Another interesting thing happened at this time. Regardless of whether the news source was politically left or right, a fake news social media stream or a traditionally objective news source, they all started to have a strange obsession with what were coined "breakthrough cases". This referred to situations in which a fully vaccinated individual would test positive for Covid. These cases created juicy headlines that attracted audiences, thereby increasing profits, so it's no wonder the topic got so much play.

Notwithstanding the popularity of these breakthrough case stories, the fact was that the vast majority of fully vaccinated people did NOT develop a breakthrough case. Breakthrough cases were not common; less than 1/10 of 1% of fully vaccinated people in the US tested positive for Covid and, among that small group, most did not experience any symptoms, some would develop only mild cold-like symptoms and far fewer would require hospitalization.[viii] Despite the sensational headlines, the reality was that it was very, very rare for a fully vaccinated person to be hospitalized or to die from Covid complications. The headlines should have read, "Unvaccinated Individuals are 11 Times More Likely to Die from Covid-19," as was the case with an article in Smithsonian Magazine written by Elizabeth Gamillo.[ix]

While some stories did lead with this sentiment, most focused on the danger of breakthrough cases. This only served to spread more fear and anxiety, making it seem like "normal life" was far off and possibly unattainable.

On September 1, 2021, Israel reported the highest number of new cases since the start of the pandemic. This was troubling, because that nation was among the first in the world to initiate widespread vaccination, with rates approaching 65% by the summer. However, what was truly frightening was the fact that for several weeks up to that point, breakthrough cases in which the elderly or infirm were dying, were occurring at increasing rates. This was a game changer and moved the talk of Covid vaccine booster shots from a casual idea to a very serious likelihood for certain patient groups. Vaccination related news quickly spiraled out of control. Some people tried to focus on the positive and were buoyed by the thought that the world was finally coming out of the woods, but this news out of Israel threatened that hope with the specter of a never-ending cycle of vaccinations. It gave reason for even greater apprehension when a significant proportion of our population refused vaccination. Once again, the anxiety machine was in full production.

Shortly after we learned of the situation in Israel, it was reported that life in other parts of the world was very, very far from returning to any semblance of normality. While millions of Americans argued about their personal freedom to choose not to avail themselves of the abundance of free vaccines, we started to become aware that, predictably, poor nations around the globe had little to no access to those same vaccines that they desperately wanted. The Center for Disease Control (CDC) continued to issue Level 4 high risk warnings for Americans to avoid travel to many popular Caribbean destinations and other nations around the globe. We all began to wonder, some aloud, some in the silence of their own thoughts, "Will the world ever get back to normal?"

Back at home, yet new concerns returned and contingencies were required as parents wondered how long it would take until their children were sent home again due to outbreaks. Different school districts across North America grappled with mask policies, distance education options and sports policies. To say it was a fluid situation would have been a gross understatement. What were parents of young children to do when their kids were sent home one week, back to school two weeks later and then were back at home four weeks after that? The distress was compounded for those parents with no babysitting, daycare or supervision options; particularly for those who during the first round worked from home, but who recently returned to the office.

While some parents were reeling from this cruel game of musical school chairs, many others were wondering about the consequences of multiple rounds of online learning; particularly for those kids who struggled with school or who simply did not have the maturity to self-motivate or self-discipline. It began looking bleak for a 2-year cohort who, collectively, might eventually be known as the "Covid Kids". There remains the potential that, due to these years of interrupted education, many of these kids may never reach their full career potential, jumping from one minimum wage job to the next. What a discouraging thought when piled on top of all of the other uncertainty surrounding this pandemic!

As recently as the U.S. Thanksgiving holiday, as masses of travelers were boarding flights to return home from family celebrations, frightening news broke about the highly mutated "Omicron" strain of Covid. Governments around the world immediately banned flights to and from South Africa and some neighboring countries; people who had recently visited the region were included in the flight ban. The swift response was considered responsible, but it put everyone around the globe on edge and made all of us question if we would ever get back to normal again.

Clearly, the world was not out of the woods and this continued to feed people's anxiety, depression and other emotion and mental illnesses. The Covid-19 pandemic left a trail of globally-experienced destruction and damage including loss of life, battered emotions, a vast political and societal divide, supply chain woes, economic uncertainty and scarred mental health.

Everyday people, businesses, politicians and even nations felt exhausted and faced a future that rarely felt so uncertain. For many, that feeling continues to linger.

Stephen J. Kristof

Chapter 2
Where Are We Now?

I would not be surprised if you feel dragged down after reading Chapter 1. Admittedly, it is a difficult but truthful perspective on a challenging and recent historical event. It's so recent that, despite being past the worst of it, we are all still dealing with remnants and reminders of the pandemic. Remember, too, that different regions in the world are still very firmly in the grips of Covid. I apologize if I have added to your stress and anxiety, but I feel that *if* progress is to be made, it's important to understand where we are and how we got here.

This chapter is about the "where we are" part. The forthcoming discussion involves some uncomfortable facts and statistics, but itemizing and examining the individual impacts of the pandemic will help you understand just why you and countless others may feel uneasy, as though your life seems unreal. It is real, I assure you, but you and I and everyone else have been through hell. I'd like to say that we've been through hell and back, but frankly, many of us aren't back yet.

Yes, we've been through a lot and it's important to reflect on the full extent of what has happened during the last few years. This is a good time for you to mentally step into this picture. When you read Chapter 1 – basically a condensed history of the Covid-19 Pandemic, what was going through your mind? Did you remember each of the events or did you forget a lot of what has transpired? Did you glide through the pandemic with eyes closed, trying to ignore the awful and potentially horrific outcomes or did the pandemic consume your every thought? Were you somehow able to cloister yourself and escape from the constant onslaught of upsetting daily lead stories about pandemic news or were you consumed by all of that noise?

For over a year and a half, most people around the globe were absorbed, at some level, into a never-ending cascade of bad news and even worse predictions. Wading through historical archives of domestic and international newspapers reveals a cycle of good/bad news about the pandemic which was like an awkward dance move; one step forward, two steps back, three steps back, one step forward, four steps back…

An analysis of television and internet news streams during the same period reveals an incidence of pandemic related lead stories that is staggering. Reflect on your own conversations with family, friends, coworkers and neighbors during that time frame. It's likely that those daily conversations included discussion about the pandemic itself, its impact on our lives, scary predictions about our future and/or tragic health news either about someone we knew or someone connected to someone we knew.

This constant barrage of bad news from virtually every angle and the inability to escape it resulted in the destruction of our emotional *"safety zones"*. Add to this the fact that, while the media and people around us kept shouting about the new normal, our lives were anything but normal. Even if someone did find a way to move happily through the pandemic (*are ignorant people really happier?*), it was pretty much impossible for most people to avoid the reality of it, because we were living it! Whether we were laid-off from our jobs, lost our jobs, worked from home, took on risk as an essential worker or suffered an endless assault as a front-line medical worker, we couldn't escape it. The grief was compounded for many parents whose children were at home trying to learn virtually on a computer and, were for the most part, hating it. Families frequently had to deal with certain family members who were not taking Covid safety seriously enough. This led to countless arguments and further increased stress.

Nearly every routine activity in our lives was transformed, from curbside pick-up of groceries to remote doctor visits to online gym workouts. Our hair grew longer and for some of us somehow lost its color. Nearly everything that could be done on a computer or phone was suddenly done that way. After the initial shock in March 2020, when store shelves abruptly became bare, we started stealthily hunting for things like toilet paper, canned goods, meats, dry goods, bottled water and anything else we thought of that might make life difficult if we ran out. In North America, as foods and products started to show up again, most people began to store small mountains of toilet paper and other items in their homes. Freezers became so overstuffed that many folks couldn't shut the door. For most of us, two years later, we still have the stockpiles to prove it and, although we don't really understand why, we keep feeding them.

During the worst parts of the pandemic – the lockdowns – we were stuck at home with a great deal of time to ruminate about how we felt life was so lousy. Then there was the travel, well, actually the lack of travel. Privileged people around the world had become so accustomed to dealing with stress or boredom by simply hopping on a plane and jetting to a relaxing or exciting destination or boarding a cruise ship to let all the worries float away. This was no longer an option. At points, jurisdictional restrictions prevented people in one state from traveling to another. In the longest ever land border travel ban, for nearly 19 months, non-essential Americans were prevented from driving beyond their borders going north or south, and, similarly, non-essential Canadians were barred from driving into the US. There really was no way of escaping what was unfolding all around us. The so-called safety zones, where one can escape the bad news, stress and reminders had simply disappeared.

Beyond the shocking but real numbers of global deaths and long-haul symptoms attributable to Covid, the virus hit us hard in other ways. It's hard to imagine how humanity got through it without a far greater cost to mental health. But the toll on mental health is only one of several impacts; this virus cost us far more than most people realize.

By late October 2021, the pandemic was responsible for the following: [x] [xi] [xii] [xiii]

- **5+ Million Deaths** *(worldwide)*

- **10 Covid Variants Identified**

- **Highest Increase in USA Poverty since 1960**

- **124 Million People, Globally, Moved Back Into Poverty** *(setting back decades of progress)*

- **Lack of "Emotional Safety Zones"**

- **Emergence of New Pandemic-Related Mental Health Issues and Suicide**

- **Increased Domestic Abuse to Children and Intimate Partners**

- **Worsening Patient Care in Areas Unrelated**

to Covid-19

- **Loss of Employment**

- **Unprecedented Damage to the Global Economy**

- **Sharp Increases in Cost of Goods, Cost of Living and Inflation**

- **Increased USA Federal Budget Deficit and Mounting Debt** *(By September 2021, the total extra US Federal spending to help mitigate the economic effects of the pandemic was nearly $4 Trillion; spending included emergency lifelines, household and employment support, and subsidies for agriculture, transportation, corporations.) *n.b. This does NOT include the $1.2 Trillion Bipartisan Infrastructure Bill that Congress passed on November 15, 2021.*

- **$11 Trillion Unexpected Spending in Financial Rescue Measures Worldwide**

We often deal with negative stressors and crises by pushing them to the back and ignoring as much as we can. However, looking at the preceding list, it's easy to see the extent to which we have been through the wringer. The pandemic has left a path of death and destruction as wide as an F5 tornado churning through a Midwest landscape. When the impacts stack up and do so for prolonged periods of time, it becomes a lot harder to mentally push them aside. The emotional toll is difficult, yet, completely predictable.

Much has been written and broadcast about this Pan-demic, but far less has been said about the "Psycho-demic," a term coined by Tom Steding, Ph.D. Most mental health illnesses and issues tend to suffer from a negative stigma; most people, including the press, simply do not want to talk about it. The mental health impact of the pandemic is no different; it has been largely underreported. This is a serious omission for two reasons. First, when the pandemic is *truly* a thing of the past, it's likely that the economic, job, transportation, supply chain and physical health issues will resolve fairly rapidly. However, we could find that the mental health problems linger for far longer. Second, the pandemic has mentally and emotionally scarred people in ways that they don't even realize, therefore these issues may not ever be effectively resolved.

It's difficult to predict accurately how and to what extent people on a global basis will continue to experience emotional and psychological fallout after the pandemic is behind us, because it has impacted our lives for far longer than we ever expected. Psychologists have studied the after-effects of modern-day major crises and catastrophes caused by things such as insurrection, political violence and natural disasters, however those types of things are geographically regional. The difference with this particular event is that it is truly global and has persisted for close to two years *(at the time of this writing)*. There has been no escape from the Covid pandemic; practically every spot on the earth knew about it, was impacted by it and continued to be impacted by it in successive waves.

In the past 50 years, there has not been a comparable event that has affected so many people so negatively and for so long.

This is a very important concept! It ties-in to why so many people have not come to terms with the trauma that they – that we all – have experienced.

Psychologists and mental health counselors report that, increasingly, they are treating patients experiencing pre-Covid and post-Covid symptoms that are similar to post-traumatic stress disorder (PTSD). So much so, in fact, that the new term "Covid PTSD" has gained wide acceptance. In a traditional understanding of PTSD, patients suffering from the disorder are often unaware that they are suffering from it. They try to go about their daily lives with much difficulty and distress, or worse, embark on a pattern of self-destruction, never knowing what is causing them to think or behave in ways that they do. In some cases, the patient is aware of what preceded or led up to the disorder, while others have buried it so deeply that it is no longer accessible on a conscious level.

Months or years after returning from military combat, surviving a serious accident or assault, recovering from a life-threatening illness or dealing with a whirlwind of stressors, PTSD can continue to challenge the simplest tasks in everyday life, and can negatively influence things like family relationships, career, physical well-being, sleep, mood and decision-making.

PTSD can also sit dormant until a trigger awakens it. It's analogous to how a person gets the Shingles later in life. In the days before the development of a chicken pox vaccine, if a child was infected with chicken pox, once the illness resolved, the varicella zoster virus hid dormant in the ganglion, potentially reawakening later in life as shingles, brought on by the trigger of a weakened immunity. This is not meant to minimize the gravity of this disorder, nor is it intended to suggest that a great swath of our population has developed something like Covid PTSD. However, it's safe to say that some people are experiencing symptoms that resemble that disorder and a majority of those people likely never considered it as a possibility.

Keep in mind that the purpose of this book is not to diagnose – or to help you self-diagnose a case of PTSD or any other mental illness! If you do believe that you suffer from any type of undiagnosed or untreated mental illness, PLEASE see a mental health practitioner for help!

The purpose of this book, instead, is to help bring some light to the _possibility_ that the Covid pandemic has impacted your emotional well-being, and to provide some tools you can use to start feeling normal again. This book is not going to solve problems in cases where pre-existing mental health issues have exacerbated one's emotional reaction to our shared Covid experience or where that experience has led to an unusually strong and negative mental health response. In such cases, proper professional diagnosis, intervention and treatment are a necessity.

On the other hand, if you are simply feeling that life is "not right," "not normal" or just hasn't returned to how it felt before the pandemic, you are not alone. This realization, in itself, can help put us on the path to better emotional balance. Many people are feeling like they really want life to seem regular or normal again and they don't understand why that hasn't happened yet. If no significant negative event has occurred in one's life since the pandemic started, then it's likely that the feeling is attributable to having dealt with a lot of change, restriction and stress for a prolonged period. Getting back to "feeling" normal sometimes isn't as easy as it seems it should be.

As noted previously, bank accounts, jobs and various freedoms (such as the freedom to travel) can be restored a lot more quickly and easily than our feelings about ourselves, our lives and the world around us. Also keep in mind that, depending on when you are reading this, we may not be entirely out of the woods yet, as far as Covid-19 is concerned. In that case, feeling normal again may take a bit longer until *all* of the regular aspects of our everyday lives, our safety, our economy and our world are back to normal. If you are reading this well after the dust has settled and it looks like everyone around you is moving ahead, consider that everyone is different and that your personal response to two years of Covid shock and stress is a highly individual thing. We all have different rates of resiliency, both mentally and physically. For example, it's similar to that coworker who rarely seems to get sick, but the odd time that they do come down with something, they seem to bounce back a day later, healthier than before! On the other hand, what about that friend who, after having the slightest injury, will invariably experience other pile-on health issues? Different people have varying degrees of resiliency.

So, where are we now? It's a bit of a trick question, because the "where" refers to different things for different people. In one respect, "where" could refer to how our lives have changed due to the pandemic. Alternatively, it could focus on the post-pandemic state of affairs in our world, our nation and our communities. Finally, "where" could have more to do with one's personal emotional state after having endured close to two years of pandemic-related restrictions and what seemed to be an endless torrent of bad news. The reality is that our current post-pandemic situation encompasses all three of these aspects.

Everyone wants life to get FULLY back to normal; not some weird "new normal", but just regular old normal. I don't think many people want to have to keep wearing masks in public places and sanitizing their hands until they are chapped and raw. You may live in a part of the world where masks have already been phased-out and you may be comfortable enough to attend packed events and indoor locations without wearing a face covering. You may be traveling once again, for business or for pleasure, and may feel at ease with boarding a plane, embarking on a cruise ship or staying at a resort. Perhaps you're fine with dining in a packed restaurant and, afterward, dancing the night away at a nightclub.

If you're doing these types of things without hesitation, it's likely that you have already resolved whatever emotional distress the pandemic brought your way. However, for every person that has reached that place, there are probably more people who have not; they have lingering concerns about the safety of doing these types of things and continue to experience turmoil and emotional distress. Put it this way; after surviving a building explosion, you wouldn't expect someone to simply get up, brush off the dust, kick the debris out of the way and just carry on. Right?

Now that we can better articulate how we got to this point and what has changed, Chapter 3 will explore the media's role. Following that, in Chapter 4, we will begin to explore our emotional selves. Once we have this awareness, we can determine the things that are within our sphere of influence and can begin working on them. For things that are beyond our control, we can at least change the way we think about them.

Chapter 3
The Media's Role

Even before the pandemic was first announced by the World Health Organization and throughout the entirety of it, we have endured a nonstop stream of mostly negative and often inflammatory news content about Covid; news that was simply devoid of hope. It's also been a considerably cruel stream of news, in that each time things started to look up, more distressing news broke out, alarming us with fear-mongering words and images related to hospitalization, ventilators, death, rising rates of infection and recurring waves that could be worse than the previous one. It's been an emotional rollercoaster – one we've all had the displeasure to ride. I've coined a new term for it; "Media Effect Psychological Whiplash".

The media bastions - traditional print and electronic news media (ie. television and radio), along with their internet properties pumped out a steady stream of Covid-related news throughout the entirety of this event; an event that we would all like to forget. However, we couldn't forget it because it was ever present. In a sense, they were just doing their jobs, but did they really need to be so sensational about it? And did it almost always have to focus on the doom, the gloom and the dread? The popular evening network television news program, "ABC World News Tonight" makes an effort to end each episode with a good news story. It's not much, but at least they set aside a few minutes out of their 20-minute show every evening to bring viewers a hopeful, good news, "warm and fuzzy" story; it's nice to end all of that stressful stuff on a positive note.

However, the reality is that throughout the pandemic – especially during upticks – we enjoyed very few of these positive breaks in the mainstream national media. Even our local television, radio and newspaper outlets continued to pound away at Covid news on a daily basis, whether they warned us about what was about to be closed, reminded us of the dreaded daily infection and death count or told us about local businesses that were failing due to the ongoing restrictions.

To make matters worse, some of the 24-hour news channels led the charge with their *ultra-repetitive* negative babble, while social media filled any remaining gaps. These sources also tend to be particularly polarizing, which is rather unsettling when we are already dealing with one of the most socially and politically divided times that most people can remember in their lives. Even as they sprinkled facts with editorial slant, some of these all-news channels, as well as countless social media blogs and podcasts hosted by so-called experts, drove an even deeper wedge into the growing political and social divide. Of course, many of these social media pundits did even more damage by selling the worst of the lies, false conspiracies and hate-driven garbage by captivatingly packaging them as "facts" and "reality". Well played, as long as you ignore the ethics; Lesson #1 from the disinformation playbook. Someone started the fire with selfish personal and political intent, and this type of media content did a tremendous job of fanning the flames.

We are now left with a rift that is all about "versus" and has nothing to do with the tenets that built and preserve freedom. The concept of political collaboration for the good of the nation now seems like a fairytale. Factions are pitted against each other with little to no middle ground. In our present society, our dedicated educators are trying to teach our children to get along and find a middle ground to solve problems; at the same time, some of their parents have been arrested at school board meetings for causing embarrassing disturbances, issuing threats of death and personal harm, fighting fiercely with those who have alternative views, and shouting belligerently at officials.

Now, full disclosure here, this is not a political book; it's a self-help book that provides many useful tools and perspectives to help people heal following a modern-day crisis that impacted most of our world's population. However, in order to do that, it's imperative to take an *honest* look at an event's history and current situation to help us better understand why we may feel the way we do.

The next part may sound politically biased, but it is not at all; this fact should be clearly obvious to *every* American regardless of political affiliation. The growing social and political divide in the US is something that began to rip apart with far greater intensity between 2017 and 2021.

<u>Sadly, the social and political divide now defines our society more than our sameness does</u>. We've rarely found ourselves living in a time when one's position on the political spectrum seems more important than one's contributions to society. What a shame!

It's not merely an embarrassment, it has also impacted our ability to overcome and heal from this pandemic, both physically and emotionally. Understand that the way you feel today, in terms of needing emotional healing, has been impacted significantly by the uncertainty and angst of living in a highly divided society. Shamelessly biased far-right media titans and dishonest pundits aggressively reinforced their lies using deep pockets and massive resources. Convinced that those lies were truth, their followers distanced themselves from everyone who didn't share their political stance, treating them like enemies and refusing to collaborate. The anxiety and emotional turmoil that these media clowns have helped create is unforgivable. Their deceit also obstructed progress in fighting Covid, challenged racial accord and eroded democratic values. It is important that everyone realizes that a portion of our emotional distress has been manufactured. The good news is that once we realize this, a path to healing becomes easier.

In terms of the previously mentioned "Media Effect Psychological Whiplash", understand that although our news streams tend to glom onto the negative, they occasionally feature a bit of positive or potentially positive news. Regrettably, it seems that the glimmer of hope is short lived. During the height of the pandemic, the media brought us an ounce of optimism and then squashed that hope with a barrel of despair. We were bounced back and forth for months on end, initially buoyed by a bit of hopeful news about the virus, just to be thrown down a deeper hole the following day. This type of coverage builds anxiety and it continues.

Here's an example; the hopeful news first. On October 19, 2021, the State of Florida was reporting that its daily case count was down by 25% from the previous week. Good news, right? It was *surprising* news to folks who supported masks and a slower opening, particularly when the state's Governor, Ron DeSantis, led an anti-masking and no restrictions effort that some feared would end in disaster. He launched legislative salvos against mandated vaccinations and masks. He even tried to prevent cruise lines operating out of Florida's ports from requiring passengers to show proof of vaccine status. By the summer, Florida's per-capita Covid cases and deaths led the nation.

However, the sudden drop in cases and deaths as reported on October 19th was cause for optimism. Whichever side of the growing political divide you were on, for once, didn't' seem to matter. With Florida's case count rapidly and inexplicably plummeting, this was good news for all of us! Finally, a glimmer of hope…

Unfortunately, the hopeful news did not last long. Later on, during that same day in October, news broke from the U.K. with a shocking reversal of hope. Following Prime Minister Boris Johnson's earlier declaration of victory over Covid, news outlets around the world reported that cases were once again soaring in Britain; so much so, that UK cases exceeded those of France, Germany, Spain and Italy combined. Johnson and DeSantis are cut from a similar political cloth, so this second story left many feeling that, as far as Florida was concerned, it was only a matter of time until the other shoe dropped in a manner similar to the U.K. experience.

As it turned out, the U.K. case count did not improve, but Florida's did. While the U.K. avoided sharp increases in Covid deaths due to their high vaccination rate, their per-capita infection rate continued to rise well into November. Other western European nations were also experiencing worrisome spikes, with some considering yet another round of lockdowns.

The news was, in a word, upsetting. We were occasionally shown a glint of hope, followed by further worry and negative news...whiplash!

A few weeks went by and Covid news seemed to settle down for a bit. Many people were starting to feel a lot more relaxed about life and more hopeful about the future. U.S. Thanksgiving arrived in late November 2021 and the nation logged the highest number of air travelers since the pandemic started. Things were looking up. Then it happened; BAM, another whiplash! The Omicron variant was identified and the news media went wild, just as those same travelers were preparing to board flights back home.

All of these external media voices have, over a 21+ month period, reinforced negative messages that left a very deep scar on all of us. In 1938, behaviorist B.F. Skinner revealed that it's relatively easy to convince someone to change their behavior by using reinforcement. Reinforcement Theory (Process Theory) has particular relevance to communication and in this context, to the media's role in covering the pandemic, while simultaneously reporting on social and political divide and unrest.

When it comes to the media's preoccupation with bad news and sensationalism, keep in mind that this is nothing new. "Yellow Journalism" is an old term describing the media's focus on sensationalism above facts; a practice that was common during the mid-to-late 1800's. It's still around; anyone who has worked in the media in modern times has heard the phrase, "When it bleeds, it leads."

It's all about getting a bigger audience; a bigger market share. It's a simple equation. The more viewers, readers or listeners you can attract, the greater the revenue that will be generated. Why the bad news? It's also simple. Although people like to say that they would rather consume good news over bad news, the reality is that bad news, especially when packaged with a sensational headline, is simply more enticing to most people. It's sort of like morbid curiosity, turning your head to see a terrible accident, even though you know it will upset you.

All of this isn't meant to be an indictment of the media in general. The media have a job to do and it would have been irresponsible to avoid covering the pandemic. Could the media have reported less on the pandemic? It would have been hard to do so when we were in the thick of it and everything in our world was ruled by Covid. Could they have been less sensational and repetitive about it? Certainly. Could they have chosen not to give credence to politicians who were espousing lies and attacking truth? Good idea, but a difficult call.

However, as noted, sensationalizing by using shockingly negative headlines, making people question reality by stating, unapologetically, that blatantly false information is true, teasing with tidbits of hope followed by the dumping of disappointing news, pushing agendas that further divide society and reinforce hopelessness...these are not part of media's role in a free and democratic society.

As you move toward healing, understand how you may have been manipulated. It's not your fault that you feel the way that you do. In a way, you may have been unknowingly programmed.

Stephen J. Kristof

Chapter 4
How Are You Feeling?

In the next 8 Sections of Chapter 4, we'll take a look at some of the most common emotional and psychological changes resulting from the pandemic. As you read ahead, ask if you see yourself in any of these scenarios. This is a necessary part of putting yourself on the path to wellness. It's one thing to say that life just doesn't feel normal anymore, but that in itself provides no starting point for repair and healing. It also leaves one in a state of stagnation with no real sense of hope or progress. A prolonged sense that life feels abnormal can also be a catalyst for bigger problems down the road, including physical and mental illness. Once we know what is *specifically* making life seem abnormal, we will be in a better position to begin addressing these problems and turning our life around.

 As we begin living in a post-pandemic world and trying to do things as "normally" as circumstances allow, we may find that nothing feels like it did before. One might experience shallowness while doing the activities that previously brought much enjoyment. We might find that we're ambivalent about the same things that used to give us a spark and that made life interesting. Things that previously brought happiness, satisfaction, challenge and fun now seem dull, empty and uninteresting. We might feel anxious for no apparent reason; even when things are going our way. Or, like so many other people these days, we have developed a new fear of being in social situations. What has happened?

There's no doubt that the world around us has changed, but is there a chance that you've also changed? It's quite likely that as the world begins to return to normal, you're not there yet and you don't know how to get back to normal. You may have been programmed by the media as noted in the last chapter. After nearly two years of dealing with how the pandemic affected your personal life, your work life, your social life, your family life and possibly even your finances, there's no question that you have changed. We all have to some degree. And that's okay. It would be unusual for someone to have gone through our collective Covid experience and not have changed in, possibly, *many* ways. As mentioned before, some individuals bounce back quickly and simply move on, never looking back, while others are not wired to be quite so resilient. And that's okay too!

So here's a look at the most common ways in which our emotional wellness and our perceptions have been changed over the last many, many months. The reasons why these changes have developed will also be explored. Try to remember as you move through this chapter that there is hope and there are many different things that you have control over that can reawaken your spirit and re-establish a sense of normalcy! Some of these things are simple and easy, while others may take a bit more of an effort, but the good thing is that feeling normal again is well within reach!

Also keep in mind that most of the tools and strategies will be discussed as you get further into this book. For now, let's get at what is causing you to feel that life isn't quite normal yet. Can you see your reflection in any of the following areas?

Emotional Impact #1
SLEEP DISORDERS

Our sleep tells us a lot about what's going on upstairs. How much sleep have you been getting lately? How has your sleep been for the past few years, especially compared to how you slept for most of your life before the pandemic? Are you experiencing or have you experienced any of the following sleep scenarios or problems in the past few "Covid Years"?

- *Waking up during the wee hours and finding it difficult to get back to sleep?*

- *Playing games on your phone at 2, 3 and 4, in the morning?*

- *Resigning to the idea that you won't sleep, so, instead you make the most of your time, reach for some coffee and read or do work instead?*

- *Surfing the internet instead of sleeping, searching for something, anything, that is reassuring?*

- *Awakening from exhausting dreams in which you are performing meaningless, yet, agonizingly repetitive tasks?*

- *Drinking increasing amounts of alcohol before going to bed to try to get a good night's sleep?*

- *Relying on sleep aids and drugs to knock yourself out?*

- *Rolling out of bed in the morning, feeling fatigued and unmotivated, despite the fact that you hit the sack at a reasonable time?*

Does any of this sound familiar? You're not alone. In fact, these insomniac experiences have become common and say a lot about one's current state of emotional health. The solution has less to do with fixing sleep than it does with fixing our thought process during our waking hours.

Now, this might sound like a trick question, but it's not. When was the last time you got a REALLY good, totally restful, full night of sleep? If you had to scratch your head and think hard to remember when that was, then the immortal words of Apollo 13 Pilot Jack Swigert come to mind: "Houston, we have a problem." *(To be honest, during that frightful moment in 1970, Swigert actually said, "Houston we've had a problem," but that just doesn't sound right!)*

If it's difficult to remember the last time you had a solid sleep, then ask yourself, honestly, what was your sleep like **before** the pandemic? It may be hard to remain objective; trying to remember what your sleep life was like two years ago might be a bit of a stretch, because we humans have a nifty way of forgetting the bad stuff the further back we go. If your sleep was actually pretty regular and restful prior to the pandemic, then it's likely that you, as with countless other people on this planet, experienced an emotional shock that continues to manifest in your sleep. The emotional shock was likely the pandemic itself (along with all of the collateral damage mentioned in the first two chapters of this book). Of course, there could be myriad other non-pandemic related situations that you faced at some point during the last two years that could also have impacted your sleep, but if nothing significant comes to mind, it is likely emotional fallout from Covid.

It could also be physical. For people who were infected with Covid and got sick from it, there may be some lingering physical illness that can alter sleep patterns. Certain ongoing "Long-Haul" Covid symptoms that may induce sleeplessness include breathing problems, muscle and joint pain, cough, chest pain, heart palpitations and a slew of other symptoms. Another problem that seems to afflict many long-haulers is ongoing or recurrent tiredness and fatigue. While that sounds contradictory *(if you're always tired, then you should be getting better sleep and more of it, right?)*, it has to do with a messed-up circadian rhythm. The best way to describe circadian rhythm, if you've never heard of it, is that it's our 24-hour internal clock that regulates sleep and waking cycles. Elderly people often have circadian issues if they nap too much through the day and, as a result, are not tired enough at night to get a solid sleep. People working swing shifts, switching from days or afternoons to nights and back again frequently experience insomnia because their circadian rhythm has been compromised.

Keep in mind that medical science cannot accurately identify the incidence of illness caused by Covid in North America during and prior to March 2020, due to the lack of testing. As a result, there may have been any number of people who contracted the illness without realizing it. Additionally, in the early months after the pandemic was formally announced, an untold number of people may have also fought the virus without feeling the need to get tested or simply avoided having a probe poked up their noses. As a result, anyone who was unknowingly infected with Covid in early 2020 could possibly be experiencing long-haul symptoms which interfere with sleep.

Speaking of disturbing one's circadian rhythm, the problem has also been observed in people who suddenly have too much time on their hands and not enough to do with it. If you were laid off from your job due to work restrictions, you may have taken advantage of the opportunity to sleep when the urge hit you and it affected your regular sleep time. Similar experiences were widely reported by those who were relocated to work from home.

For many, Covid has also led to job loss or major career change, both of which can impact sleep negatively. Additionally, many previously harmonious families have been challenged for many pandemic-related reasons, leading to disagreements, fighting, abusive behaviors and frustration; all of which can lead to many sleepless nights.

When you see how many different ways Covid can create sleep problems, it's likely that most people have been impacted. It's also a very important problem to tackle. In May 2006, the American Journal of Managed Care published a study by Dr. Karl Doghramji that confirmed how insomnia contributes to poor health and shortens life expectancy.[xiv] Many other studies have affirmed this relationship. If your sleep continues to be impacted negatively due to Covid-related or other reasons, addressing this problem is an obvious priority.

As for those crickets and their nightly serenade, they don't always do the trick. Alas, if your sleep has been impacted negatively related to this virus, consider yourself in good company. <u>Chapter 5, Tool #2, has some easy to apply and extremely effective strategies to help repair your sleep life</u>.

Emotional Impact #2
MALAISE

Malaise - it's a fancy way of describing a state of mind that is, well, in the dumps. Lack of energy, pessimism, mildly depressed thoughts, struggling to find the bright side of things, low self-motivation; these are the ingredients for a nasty soup called Malaise. "Covid Malaise" is actually a thing now and many mental health practitioners are well versed in its diagnosis and treatment options. Everyone feels malaise at times during their lives and, for some, it even graces us with weekly visits. For most, these episodes are short lived and minor in nature. However, for some people, malaise is part of a broader mental health issue.

IF you've lived with malaise-type symptoms for an extended period of time, regardless of Covid, and you have never had a related diagnosis, you need to bring this to the attention of your family doctor. Several physical conditions are associated with these symptoms. If your doctor provides a diagnosis and feels that the cause is of mental health origin, he or she can provide further referral to a suitable practitioner. If you already have a relationship with a mental health practitioner, that professional needs to be aware of these symptoms.

IF your symptoms are severe and debilitating or if you have had suicidal ideation (thoughts, even fleeting, of suicide) you need to access medical and/or psychological help urgently.

If you are having suicidal thoughts, please call or text a suicide prevention hotline immediately. **If you reside in the US, call the National Suicide Prevention Lifeline by dialing 9-8-8**. Alternatively, dial 1-800-273-8255 or Text GO to 741741 to reach a trained Crisis Counselor; the service is free and available 24/7.

If you reside in Canada, call The Canada Suicide Prevention Service at 1-833-456-4566, available 24/7, or text a message to 45645 (4pm to midnight ET). If you reside in other international locations, please search and contact the closest suicide hotline using the following website directory:

http://www.suicide.org/international-suicide-hotlines.html

However, if your malaise type symptoms are troublesome, but not severe, and have come on concurrently with the arrival or continuation of Covid and you have had no other major negative change in your life, you may be experiencing Covid Malaise. If Covid has left you feeling in the dumps you are not alone. There are many reasons why Covid has spawned malaise and they include:

- *Social and Physical Isolation*
- *Lack of Productive/Creative Challenge*
- *High Levels of Stress*
- *Constant Cycle of Bad News and Worse News*
- *Lack of Hope for Improvement (ie., "The New Normal is here to stay)*
- *Staying Home and Not Getting Out or Going to Work*
- *Long Term and Recurring States of Emergency*
- *Not Working or Working in Unusual Circumstances (ie., working from home)*
- *Lack of Usual Social and Recreational Past Times or Sports*
- *Constant Worrying*
- *Lack of Physical Exercise*
- *Not Seeing a Way Forward*

Any one of these factors, alone, may not be enough to constitute prolonged malaise. However, when we experience several of them simultaneously and they begin stacking on top of one another without resolution, malaise often develops.

What made matters worse in terms of this pandemic, is the fact that, unlike a major weather event such as a snowstorm or ice storm which usually lasts only a day or two, this pandemic wore out its welcome a LONG time ago! When we consider how our lives were altered so significantly for over a year and a half, it's no wonder that a societal and individual malaise developed. This has been more like a hurricane, massive flood or wildfire which changed peoples' lives for many, many months.

As with all of these negative impacts of Covid, there are, fortunately, things that we can do and behaviors that we can alter – some quite easily – which have the potential to make a significant improvement in our disposition and in finding our way back to 'normal'.

As you move through this chapter, continue to keep an open mind to some other ways that this pandemic may have influenced your emotional state. Hope is around the corner, both in terms of the pandemic's eventual end and in terms of how you can take control of your current response to what has been a very tough time for all.

Emotional Impact #3
WORRY AND ANXIETY

When it comes to your personality, how are you known by others? If a stranger were to ask your family, your social friends, your neighbors and your colleagues about your personality, what types of traits would we hear consistently in their responses? Would we hear that you are optimistic, bubbly, happy-go-lucky, talkative and supportive? Or would we hear that you tend to be a bit of a recluse, overanalyze things too deeply, focus on potentially negative outcomes, focus on yourself and worry too much about everything? Oh my, such generalizations! Fortunately, we human beings are far more complex than these two oversimplified profiles.

After that bit of levity, though, how *would* they describe your personality? Specifically, what would they say about the way that you deal with stress and potentially negative outcomes? It's interesting how two children born and raised in the same family, experiencing pretty much the same things, can have such divergent personalities! We've all seen this; you likely know of an example or two within your own extended family. Sometimes we see it as early as infancy. One child is a worrywart, becoming unhinged when the slightest thing goes wrong; the other one steamrolls over everything in its path.

Sociologists believe that our personalities are determined by our physical environment, our culture, our experiences and heredity. This is true for many aspects of our personalities; there's no doubt that our environment and culture can influence our personality. Additionally, elements of our character change or evolve as we move through life and experience different things. However, these things don't account for the example given above, where different children from the same family, with the same physical environment, the same culture, the same heredity and very similar experiences have lifelong personality traits that are so different from one another.

Some people explain this by taking a metaphysical approach, speculating that we choose our personality before God breathes life into us. Others take a scientific approach, suggesting that our personality is determined by our brain physiology. Then there are those who believe that our personalities are based merely on luck of the draw.

Regardless of exactly what factors are responsible for our personalities, consider that you *are* likely predisposed to react and respond in a certain way to negative circumstances and uncertainty. You already know this about yourself! Therefore, when we drill down beyond the façade, past the bravado, behind the face we show to our coworkers and neighbors, what do you look like? If you are a worrier, if you're inclined toward anxiety, if you try to push uncomfortable upcoming events to the back of your mind, then there's no question that the stress and uncertainty created by this extended pandemic has had an especially hard impact on your anxiety.

By the way, if you do have a habit of ignoring and burying your stresses and anxieties from conscious thought, you should realize that it's almost impossible to get away with. Although you may initially distract yourself with other thoughts and activities, the reality is that your subconscious mind and a good part of your conscious mind have awareness of what you have tried to bury. It invariably bubbles up and spoils your peace of mind.

If you realize that you are intrinsically a worrier, you may have discovered that there's been an add-on to your state of mind since the pandemic. Like many, you may suddenly feel anxious from time-to-time for no particular reason. Perhaps you're not able to deal as effectively with as many different stresses as you could prior to the pandemic? A common complaint in this post-pandemic period is that people feel overwhelmed, even though some admit to having fewer pressures to deal with than they had before the pandemic. There's no doubt that the constant focus on Covid has exposed a raw nerve. Imagine scratching a patch of skin on your arm over and over again during a two-year period. That area would become raw, irritated, inflamed and sore to the touch. Now, try to visualize your built-in ability to process and cope with negative situations and fears as an emotional version of that same patch of skin. Get it?

We all worry about the future, approach new situations with a certain amount of trepidation and would rather not deal with the unknown. However, we're all different in terms of the degree to which we feel these things. Some of us are much better at it and some of us are much worse at it. However, if this area happens to be one of your weaknesses, **it's very important that you realize it's not your fault!** That bears repeating; your tendency toward worry and anxiety can simply have a lot to do with what you've observed through your culture and parental role modeling. The fix may be as simple as equipping you with tools that you were never exposed to or given. Your chronic worry and resultant anxiety can also have something to do with how you're wired. Just like an electronic device that has shorted-out or that's performing unexpectedly, there are fixes; sometimes quite simple, but extremely effective fixes that can be applied. In terms of these types of fixes, a primary fix has to do with coping skills.

Your raw and irritated patch of anxiety could also have developed over an extended period of time prior to the pandemic. Common real-life experiences that can result in this feeling include ongoing stressful situations, such as being a primary caregiver for a very ill or dying loved one, working in an environment with unrelenting stress and pressure or trying to help a family member with severe mental illness and/or addiction. These are just a few examples of circumstances that can elevate our anxiety to an ongoing state of hypersensitivity. If you see yourself in this realm, keep in mind that the pandemic likely exacerbated your already raw anxiety. Again, it's not your fault.

Understanding that you have done your best to cope with and get through difficult times is a productive first step. Having the willingness to learn new proven coping skills and to follow through on applying them can do wonders for one's anxiety, much like applying a soothing balm to that irritated patch of skin.

Some effective coping strategies are discussed later in this book in Chapter 5, Tool #1.

Emotional Impact #4
COVID PTSD

The emergence of Covid PTSD was touched upon earlier, and it is a very real burden that many people are experiencing; for a portion of them, their Covid PTSD symptoms have <u>not</u> been diagnosed. If your individual experience with Covid was traumatic and you are aware that it has resulted in a serious or debilitating psychological response, also as noted previously, you should seek help from a qualified mental health practitioner, because significant symptoms in this regard or actual PTSD illness requires professional mental health treatment and management. It is not something that you can or should self-treat. Be aware that, for many people, Covid-related trauma has created PTSD-like symptoms; they may even continue to come to light as we move toward a post-pandemic stage.

<u>Some of the common symptoms of this disorder include</u>:

- *Intrusive memories of the traumatic event (during sleep or sometimes percolating into daytime thoughts)*

- *Not being able to think logically*

- *Experiencing "triggers" that set you off; sometimes in extreme or unpredictable ways*

- *Not being able to move past the trauma*

- *Hyperarousal to ordinary stimuli*

- *Avoidance behaviours*

- *Unpredictable mood swings*

It's impossible to diagnose yourself with PTSD, but it can be valuable to know the general causes and type of symptoms. Keep in mind that for a professional to diagnose PTSD, the patient would experience these types of symptoms for over a month, to a degree where they would interfere with daily life, quality of life and relationships. Seeing a professional mental health practitioner for all emotional and mental health issues is always recommended.

There are many ways that, globally speaking, Covid left deep scars on individuals and the trauma in some cases was acute. Covid PTSD cases are most often associated with losing a loved one, personally surviving a Covid infection or working in certain frontline occupations.

Sorrowfully, Covid robbed the lives of so many of our loved ones, friends and coworkers. When we lose a loved one or a very close friend, the experience can be traumatic beyond our conscious realization. What makes matters worse with Covid, is that, whether or not we contracted or became ill with the disease, we still experienced the upheaval of the pandemic itself, which compounded the trauma of losing a loved one to it. It's like the difference between when someone dies alone in a motor vehicle accident and if you were in that same vehicle with them. The trauma from losing someone to a Covid-related death was compounded by the worldwide pandemic itself.

Another factor that exacerbated the trauma was the fact that, for the most part, surviving relatives were not permitted to be with their loved ones before and during the time of their passing. The helplessness of knowing that your family member or close friend is dying and there's nothing you can do about it is heartbreaking. However, experiencing this sorrow while being forbidden from being with them during their final hours feels so inhumane. What a traumatic experience, indeed.

Another group that tends to have significant incidence of Covid PTSD are the individuals who became seriously ill from the disease. One-third of all Covid cases in which the patient developed the sensation of not being able to breathe, resulted in clinically-diagnosed PTSD.[xv] For patients who survived serious infection, whether an individual was ultimately intubated, was transferred to intensive care, stayed in hospital for an extended period of time or developed chronic long-haul symptoms, the trauma could be considered extreme. Coming so close to death or losing total control over one's physical body for an extended period of time is emotionally harrowing; the relief of surviving such an ordeal may not be the final phase of one's healing. In such cases, one's mental health also needs treatment and time to heal.

Others who, during the pandemic, were exposed to traumatic circumstances include front line workers and, with special emphasis, workers and professionals in health care environments. While most people were distraught because they had to work from home, couldn't go away for a vacation or had to change the way they shopped, healthcare employees lived a daily and relentless ordeal for close to two years. These very special members of our society gave so much of themselves, day after day, without being able to separate themselves from the trauma that continued to occur all around them. Many of them also lived in fear of unintentionally passing the virus to loved ones. The Covid-related incidence of anxiety, depression and PTSD in healthcare workers around the world is understandably staggering.

If you have or suspect that you have developed a PTSD type of response to your particular Covid experience, get professional help; this advice is echoed often in this book. Treat it seriously. If you have been diagnosed with PTSD and are presently in treatment, your mental health professional may be using a regime which includes Cognitive Behavioral Therapy, Cognitive Processing Therapy and/or Exposure Therapy. He or she may follow another treatment regime based on your individual needs. Follow your practitioner's therapeutic plan and give yourself time to heal. You may also have been prescribed a serotonin medication to help reduce the sense of threat and fear. Again, follow their professional treatment plan. *(This book does not provide individual professional advice or endorse any particular treatment; as mentioned several times, if you suspect that you may have a mental health issue or mental illness, see a professional mental health practitioner for an accurate and proper diagnosis, and treatment plan.)*

If you are merely dealing with difficulty coping with a Covid-related event but do not suspect that it has advanced to actual PTSD, there are things that you can do that will help you find your way back to a more comfortable mindset.

Try to rebuild your social network. Safely reengage with friends and with life in general. If you have been removed from your traditional work environment and continue to work remotely, consider an opportunity to relocate back to the traditional workplace when it becomes available. As our world opens-up again, so are renewed opportunities for socialization and recreation. Join a new club or sport, or start attending one you had enjoyed prior to the pandemic.

For many people, after isolating and maintaining social distance from family and friends, they somehow stopped talking and fell through the cracks. These folks were left behind once restrictions were loosened and now feel bitter for being abandoned. If you recognize yourself in this description, try not to harbor any ill will toward your family, friends, coworkers or associates who may seem to have deserted you. Due to the dynamics of repeated lockdowns and social restrictions, everyone has had difficulty finding their place and it has been an exceptionally common situation for people to be accidentally left behind. If you feel that this has happened to you, reconnect with these people; try to ignore your feelings of abandonment and swallow your pride. Remind yourself that you may actually have been the one who was not ready to renew in-person socializing as soon as they were. Forgive them silently, say nothing more about it and make the first step toward reconnecting with them. This is the healthiest thing that you can do. Consider that safe person-to-person contact is far more therapeutic than when it occurs remotely, so get back in the real-life social game!

Having said this, there are far fewer, but still some, situations in which a previously close social friend took advantage of the opportunity provided by the pandemic to break off that friendship and move in a new social direction. If you feel abandoned by everyone, it's more likely that you simply fell through the cracks, as did so many other people. However, if there is only one or a few individuals who have made themselves unavailable to you, there is the chance that they have decided to move on. Don't assume that this is the case! Initiate contact. You may find that they, just like you, have not been comfortable in fully engaging on a social basis and you can take it from there.

However, if this former friend continues to remain distant, cold and unavailable, you may have to accept that they have actually moved on. Perhaps the relationship was not as gratifying for them as it was for you, you did not share as much in common as you thought or they are simply using a "page break" to take their own life in a completely different direction. If this is true, allow them to make a clean break; you need to move on as well. Continuing to pursue a friendship at this point is futile and will not result in anything positive for either of you. It will also drag you down a path that's increasingly difficult to return from emotionally. The advice in this circumstance is to preserve your self-esteem, and seek out new friendships with people who are supportive, have a genuine interest in your welfare and who have a lot in common with you.

When you begin meeting with your friends once again, remove the mask of bravado that says, "I'm doing fine." They will be far more supportive and helpful to your overall healing if you are open and honest. Plus, you will find the process of reconnecting to be far less difficult without putting on an act and worrying about what you sound and look like.

Confide in those who are good for you and who genuinely care about you.

Traumatic events can be difficult to move beyond. If you experienced a traumatic event during this pandemic, it may be more difficult to process or cope with than had it occurred during normal times. If you are having difficulty dealing a particular memory or set of memories, try to see them as they are; merely memories of the events and not the events themselves. Sometimes people experience more anxiety by trying to avoid remembering a traumatic or difficult event than they actually have in thinking about and processing it. While facing your fears rather than running away from them, you may also think about things that have previously brought you enjoyment as well as new things that you might want to try out. You're not trying to replace the nasty memories, but instead, taking the initiative to introduce comforting new thoughts and experiences that diminish the priority you've given to the discomforting ones.

In a sense, it's much like working through the stages of grief when dealing with the death of a loved one. If one focuses too much attention on the death itself, its cause or the final moments, it creates a highly negative mindset; so much so, that it can colour or paint over the happy memories of that person. By thinking more about those joyful memories and what your loved one meant – and still means – to you, their death becomes less relevant than the goodness of who they were.

When you start taking life by the reins again and living it more fully, you introduce a flood of healthy and positive thoughts that create balance and emotional wellbeing.

Emotional Impact #5
BOREDOM WITH WHAT WAS PREVIOUSLY INTERESTING

What are you doing these days that you enjoy? Are you finding that the things that were interesting and pleasurable prior to the pandemic continue to carry the same degree of appeal or have they somehow become dull and tedious? Think about your work, pastimes, hobbies, socializing, recreation, cooking, gardening and, yes, even housework. Are these activities as enjoyable as they used to be? The experience of deriving far less pleasure from previously enjoyable activities was a very common complaint voiced during the height of the pandemic, but this disinterest has continued for many individuals. What happened?

There are several reasons for this phenomenon, but there's no doubt the pandemic bears a great deal of responsibility. In the first place, remember that due to lockdowns and restrictions, many of us were stuck at home for extended periods of time, reliving the frustration as we moved from one wave to the next. When we were stuck at home, we weren't able to get out and enjoy many of our beloved outdoor leisure and recreation activities. On top of that, some of our homes became very small and uncomfortable, as people who were forced to work from home reassigned parts of their living quarters to become makeshift offices. The leftovers, in terms of restricted activities and limited space in which to do them, felt more like crumbs than leftovers; those crumbs got tired and boring fairly quickly. The boredom became even more unbearable for people whose favorite activities normally involve other people. If you're the type of person who thrives in remote outdoor and/or social settings, you probably found the pandemic far more emotionally draining than someone who is very happy being a homebody.

When your options become greatly reduced – as happened with the pandemic – what's left over becomes boring and repetitive. Instead of spending a reasonable amount of time playing video games, watching movies, completing crosswords, finishing tasks around the home and doing whatever home-based hobby you may have, most of us found ourselves devoting enormous amounts of time to singular, repetitive activities.

When something that was previously captivating is no longer even interesting, it often leaves us feeling unfulfilled, bored and unmotivated. Another reason why certain activities may no longer be interesting for you is that they may have lost their purpose. For example, keeping your home tidy doesn't sound like a very enjoyable part of most people's lives, but most of us really like the outcome. It feels a lot better returning to a well-organized, clean and tidy home than one that looks *(and smells?)* like a pigpen! But when we're no longer hosting family dinners, big traditional holiday celebrations or entertaining social friends, we might wonder, "What's the purpose of keeping my house in tip-top shape?"

As a result, keeping the house tidy has become very low on the priority list for many people who found the practice to be fulfilling before the pandemic. The same attitude applies to yard work, gardening and outdoor home maintenance. While some folks would rather watch college football or basketball every Saturday, others can't wait to get out and work in the yard. Some people in the latter group have experienced the same onset of disinterest in outdoor work despite having an initial spark during the initial stages of the pandemic.

Stores selling home improvement, landscaping and outdoor living goods had revenues shoot through the roof in 2020 and

2021. This corporate shot in the arm was directly attributable to the pandemic. People were stuck at home and, because they were not going on expensive vacations, had more discretionary income. Much of that money went into the home.

However, despite this flurry of activity, for many people it was a flash in the pan; soon after fixing their homes and doing the work, they quickly became bored and tired of it, losing their interest in renovations, yard work and upkeep. It was interesting to walk, cycle or drive around neighboring properties, to compare the level of creativity and effort that homeowners invested in their exteriors and landscaping from 2020 to 2021. After the first round of lockdowns in spring of 2020, clarity sunk in that summer travel was simply not going to happen. Homeowners were so bored of being stuck inside and having nothing to do, that they jumped at the opportunity to spruce-up their home exteriors and landscaping; projects that a lot of those same people never had any interest in doing prior to the pandemic. By the summer of 2021, the novelty wore off and many of these homeowners opted for less work compared to the previous summer. They were just bored…like everyone.

In March 2020, CNBC conducted an online poll of just under 9,000 American workers and found that, surprisingly, 85% of them were happy with their jobs.[xvi] Unfortunately, the pandemic robbed many workers of something they found was an important and variably enjoyable part of their lives. Droves of employees were laid off – some permanently – in hospitality, retail, service and other sectors of our economy. Others were reassigned to work from home.

The idea of working from home initially sounded like an awesome idea for many workers in vastly different occupations and professions, but as time moved on, most of those same workers found the experience to be unfulfilling. Many couldn't wait to get back to the regular workplace, while others adjusted to their new digs and found that they preferred working from home. If you were assigned to work 'remotely' and grew to dislike it, you're in a very big club.

Many in this situation found that the loss of structure and social environment reduced their motivation to do what was previously enjoyable, while others despised the fact that they were forced to sacrifice needed space, retrofitting part of their home for a makeshift office. Remote meetings became the norm and, for a wide swath of the workforce, this continues to be the way they are doing business. At the same time, conducting meetings, consultations and teaching over virtual video conferencing platforms like Zoom, Google Meet, Microsoft Teams and Cisco's Webex, among others, created new challenges. While the opportunity to conduct virtual online meetings represents a truly remarkable technology, it can be challenging to say the least, for many users. The bottom line is that for countless individuals, one of the very important and enjoyable parts of their lives was impacted greatly by this pandemic.

(If on the other hand you were or are still working remotely due to the pandemic and love it, hopefully you will continue to have the opportunity to do so. However, now that the pandemic is starting to appear in the rear-view mirror, a lot of home-based workers are being called back and this is creating significant challenges for many of those workers and for their employers. We are now facing a situation – a real threat to our economy – wherein many workers are choosing to quit rather than return to the workplace. In 2021, tens of millions of American workers chose to leave their jobs due to pandemic-related reasons and, depending on which study you read, up to a quarter of all workers have said that they were planning to leave their jobs at the end of the pandemic. Even more surprisingly, up to 75% of all workers are re-thinking their skill sets due to the pandemic.)

The systemic boredom brought on by the pandemic has also touched the way we dress, our personal hygiene and even our hairstyles. As you go about your daily routines, look at other people in your environment. How's their overall appearance? It seems that A LOT of people have lost their sense of style; what's worse is that they just don't seem to care. So many people in workplaces, out shopping and in just about any public place are pushing the limits on what's considered casual. There is a big difference between appearing casual but appropriate for social settings – and – appearing casual in a way that should not ever be seen outside of the home. Let's get this straight, this discussion is merely about outward appearance; perhaps society placed too much weight on the superficial prior to the pandemic. That being said, we have a problem when folks go to work or even just out and about in public, without showering, combing their hair or wearing appropriate apparel. There's an even deeper problem than that; lack of attention to our outward appearance impacts our personal self-image. That's not a good thing at all.

In terms of life skills and meeting societal norms, teachers have always strived to instill in their pupils the importance of personal image. Our outward appearance shouldn't matter to others, just as we should not judge anyone based on their appearance. However, when we no longer care about how we look because we've lost interest in it, what kind of example are we setting for our children, for our coworkers and for society in general? When we let ourselves go to the extent that we're not meeting expected standards in the workplace, this absolutely does impact our personal potential for advancement and possibly even our ability to remain employed. Similarly, when our hygiene, attire and other elements of outward appearance leave us looking unkempt, sloppy and scruffy, what kind of message are we sending to others about our own standards and about how we feel about ourselves? Whether or not it's true, we may be sending out a message that we just don't care about anything anymore, that we're having serious financial difficulty or that our self-esteem is quite low.

Every family is different and has their own standards in many different areas. However, imagine a family in which, traditionally, everyone dresses up for the big holidays and celebrations. Next, picture a male member of that family showing up for Christmas dinner wearing wrinkled and odorous sweatpants, along with a tattered t-shirt that has mustard and ketchup stains on it. As you give a quick up-and-down eyeball to "Cousin Eddie", it's also hard not to notice his long and disheveled hair, and his five o'clock shadow. What kind of message does this guest's personal appearance send to the host and everyone else in attendance? Clearly, everyone else in the family would feel disrespected and would likely wonder if this relative is battling a significant personal or mental health issue.

In summary, if you've found that you're just not feeling the spark doing things that were previously interesting and enjoyable, explore some new hobbies, pastimes and opportunities for recreation. Put yourself out there. Clean the house, inside and out, whether you want to or not – you will regain interest in tidying, organizing, mowing the lawn, etc., once you see how good everything looks! Pay attention to your personal hygiene every day – even on your days off and even if you're not working or attending school. If you can afford it, invest in a wardrobe update. Buy something that is more stylish than what you've been wearing. If you started bribing your daughter, son or spouse to cut and style your hair because your stylist was closed, it's *way* past time to go back to your hairdresser! That distinct line between old colored hair and new grey hair is not called "ombre" and, frankly, looks awful! If you previously enjoyed personal spa services like massages, manicures, facials, pedicures and such, give them a whirl again. It's highly unlikely that you will dislike them now.

If you lost your job due to the pandemic, and feel bored and dejected, it's time to get to work. Any work. The longer you wait, the longer the gap in your resume; most prospective employers would rather see that you did *something* productive with your time rather than nothing while waiting for the "right job". Volunteer, network, put yourself in motion. If you are employed, but have lost interest in your job or even in your occupation, then do some skills and interest inventories and start making a plan for your future. Perhaps this is the right time to reinvent yourself or to find something that's a better fit for you now and into the future. This pandemic has made many people question what they are doing with their lives. It has also made many people aware of the fact that they hate *what* they do for a living or *who* they work for. **Life is short; explore the options and put a plan in place.**

**Regret is the most bitter of all pills
for one to swallow later in life.**

As you reengage with life in different ways, you'll find that many of the things that used to bring you pleasure will do that once again. For some activities, you may have to revamp and change things up; maybe a change was long overdue. As you develop new interests, your enjoyment of life in general will increase and your mood will improve in step. Maybe it's time to reinvent an aspect of yourself; again, maybe that is long overdue as well!

As you care, once again, for your outward appearance and that of your home, your self-esteem will improve as well. **In short, start living life again and you will find that *everything* becomes more interesting!**

Emotional Impact #6
LACK OF MOTIVATION AND CONSTANT STATE OF FATIGUE

Believe it or not, one of the most common complaints during the pandemic was that of feeling fatigued along with a lack of motivation to do, well, anything. If you felt that way or you're still experiencing it, you're not alone. The reasons are diverse, but they include: job loss, being bored of everything (as discussed in the last Section), lack of meaningful challenge, frustration with an awful state of affairs *(the pandemic and how it changed our lives)* aggravation with the fact that we could not control our environment, disappointment over cancelled vacations and celebrations *(even weddings)*, lack of socialization, reduced opportunities for recreation and physical movement, diminished mental stimuli, and enduring an extended period of bad and worse news with little apparent hope for resolution.

One additional factor that has contributed to the ongoing fatigue that many people are experiencing, has to do with a rather common aspect of post-Covid recovery. Some people who were diagnosed and became ill with this virus have experienced a very challenging road to recovery; those experiencing Post-Covid Fatigue syndrome are sometimes referred to as "Long Haulers". These individuals may find that their symptoms last for months and even years. An article published in late 2020 in Brain Sciences Journal revealed that of all of the many ongoing symptoms experienced by those who have recovered from

Covid-19, "Fatigue is one of the most persistent and debilitating."[xvii]

Keep in mind that the number of undiagnosed cases of illness from this virus, both domestically and globally, is unknown and will likely always remain that way. Think back to early 2020 before people and authorities knew anything about this new virus. There were so many personal anecdotal accounts of individuals getting sick from what many described as, "...the worst cold or flu I've ever had." Whether or not the Covid-19 Coronavirus was responsible for those illnesses will never be known, because either an accurate test was not yet available or, later on, the patient never bothered to get tested.

While the knowledge pool about Long-Haul syndrome is still growing and evolving, it's becoming clear that the ongoing symptoms are complex and that fatigue is one of the most common complaints. It can also impact different people in different ways. Recovery time is unknown and the extent to which it can affect different body systems varies with the person. Pre-existing conditions can also influence the extent to which Long-Haul symptoms interfere with daily functioning. What doctors and other medical professionals *do* know about this chronic aftermath illness, is that there are certain therapies that may help, such as physiotherapy, breathing exercises and other modalities, based on the patient's condition. In other words, those experiencing fatigue and diminished energy should seek medical attention to identify suitable medical interventions.

Stephen J. Kristof

Emotional Impact #7
FEAR OF DOING ORDINARY THINGS

A curious thing is happening as our world slowly recovers from the pandemic; a pandemic that is no longer *completely* strangling economies, transportation systems, supply chains and peoples' liberties. Granted, many of these factors continue to be impacted, but they do appear to be getting better. Looking around, it's clear that some of these impacts may continue to be felt for some time; delays for shipping containers arriving at ports or waiting to leave them, and the potential for runaway inflation are just two examples. However, the reality is that a lot of our various systems are actually far better than they were a year ago.

For the longest time, people everywhere were singing a common chorus of, "I can't wait to be able to travel, dine out and just do everyday things again!" However, as the opportunity to fully partake in these activities has started to return, many people are just not ready. In fact, they are downright fearful of engaging, once again, in the activities that they previously enjoyed and really looked forward to doing. We feel especially weak, gutless and timid when we see our friends and family members getting out and living life fully, while we continue to harbor fear of infection. It doesn't seem fair and it's difficult to deal with the mixed messages. On one hand, we continue to hear public health officials' collective focus on safety, while at the same time, most things have opened-up. It's confusing and disconcerting.

By September 1, 2021, only 11 US states continued to have mask mandates, although individual cities and counties had their own requirements. Meanwhile, in Canada, almost half of the nation was still required to wear masks in public areas, a mandate that had overwhelming public support. By the beginning of October, the Canadian Hub for Applied and Social Research at the University of Saskatchewan was reporting that 8 in 10 Canadians supported mask mandates in schools[xviii]. At the same time, a majority of Americans still supported mask mandates in schools, but by a lower margin. On a global scale, mask mandates and vaccination rates varied widely. Some countries basically gave up on masks and decided to let things take their course; the United Kingdom, Denmark, Norway, Finland and Sweden removed mask mandates, with Germany and France retaining the mandates for adults, but not requiring masks for school children.

One of the most compelling reasons that people had (and are continuing to experience) a fear of doing what used to be considered ordinary things is, quite simply, because the pandemic is not yet resolved. There is no such thing as universal progress around the globe when it comes to Covid. While some jurisdictions appear to be well on their way to eradicating the disease, others are just starting what will be a very long and arduous process. It's quite literally all over the place.

Fear of doing ordinary things is stoked by uncertainty that remains. By November 2021, there was a strange jigsaw puzzle of mask and vaccine requirements in the US and around the world, depending on where and what was involved. While masks were not required in public in most US states, the CDC required masks to be worn during the duration of all flights and other forms of public transportation in the US, including trains, buses and even subways. While some states were fully open, others were still experiencing worrisome surges; by mid-November, the state of Michigan, for example, had experienced growing numbers of infections since the summer, with infectious disease experts and hospital executives publicly voicing concerns about families and friends gathering for upcoming Thanksgiving and Christmas celebrations. Who would have thought last year, that a full year later, we would still be dealing with many of the same concerns about celebrating with friends and family? As Michigan was bracing itself for a fourth Covid wave, the University of Michigan had experienced a sudden outbreak of the seasonal flu that was so severe, the CDC was sent to investigate.[xix] Just days before Thanksgiving, several Michigan hospitals were reporting overcapacity, with some patients waiting on gurneys in hallways. Things were not looking very settled for the state.

Let's compare what was happening in Michigan with that of a Western European nation half way around the world; this illustrates just how much various parts of the world differed in terms of their individual Covid response. By mid-November 2021, Michigan had an unimpressively low vaccination rate of only 63% *(12 years and older)* with little movement on the dial and few options to motivate unvaccinated residents to get both jabs. Meanwhile, Austria had a slightly higher, but also poor vaccination rate of 65%; it was one of the lowest rates in Western Europe. The striking difference between Michigan and Austria was in how the two jurisdictions dealt with the threat that unvaccinated individuals posed to fully vaccinated folks; a threat to people who did their duty and rolled-up their sleeves.

While Michigan watched its vaccination rate stagnate and its infection rate balloon, the state government's hands were tied; nothing much more than public education and advertising could be instituted to at least try to change the picture. By contrast, Austria introduced a very strict lock-down for citizens who failed to get vaccinated, with the exception of those under 12 and those who had recently recovered from Covid illness. The move wasn't without criticism and even condemnation from both inside and outside Austria, with some calling the new law unconstitutional.[xx] Constitutional or not, the policy illustrated just how differently the world was approaching the seemingly never-ending scourge of Covid.

Understand that Austria's government is not all that dissimilar to that of the U.S. Just like the U.S., Austria is a democracy with a constitution and three branches of government; Executive, Legislative, and Judicial. Austria uses a bicameral parliamentary system with both a President and a Chancellor; otherwise, it is a free country very much like any other well-established democracy. However, when we compare what was going on in one U.S. state – Michigan – with Austria, we see an entirely different method of dealing with the same problem of having too many unvaccinated citizens.

In no way is this to suggest that Austria's somewhat heavy-handed response was superior to Michigan's or, for that matter, to the federal response from the U.S. Nevertheless, it does effectively illustrate the disparity in philosophy and public policy in terms of the balancing act between freedom and safety. Austria's novel and extreme response provides greater protection for those who did get vaccinated, but it may appear to many as being punitive. From a North American perspective, it seems rather harsh and even authoritarian to give police the power to do spot checks to ensure that people out in public places are double-vaccinated, along with the authority to apply further penalty or punishment. Even if the Austrian policy proved to be effective in squeezing the unvaccinated into getting their vaccinations and reducing Covid infections, it's highly unlikely that Americans and Canadians would ever support such a policy.

Further around the globe, also in November 2021, Singapore announced that it would stop paying for medical bills related to Covid treatment for any of its citizens who refused to get vaccinated and were subsequently sickened by it. Again, we see a different country and yet a very different strategy.

As much as we wanted it to be in the rear-view mirror, the pandemic was not completely there. When Covid cases, hospitalizations and deaths began spiking again in the U.K. following that nation's lifting of all restrictions and mask requirements, it created doubt and worry about the outcome of similar relaxation of rules in the US and elsewhere.

When we look at how out-of-step everything feels around the world, in terms of Covid policies and progress, it's easy to feel confused about where things stand as far as how safe it is to start living life fully and without concern of infection! Prior to Thanksgiving, we continued to receive contradictory advice that didn't exactly bolster our confidence. Take, for instance, attending sporting events. The NFL did not require fans to mask-up, although they recommended it, while individual teams and stadiums had varying policies for spectators, in terms of masks and vaccination. College football in the US had a strange mish-mash of requirements, although players, staff and coaches who were not playing on the field needed to wear masks. In terms of NHL hockey games, there was no consistency, with some teams and arenas enforcing strict vaccination and mask requirements for all spectators, staff and players, while other venues didn't bother to check spectators for vaccination status and masks were a personal choice. Further confusing the landscape was the fact that some fans supported protective restrictions, while others reeled against them.

By late 2021, most churches, temples, mosques and other places of worship were open for in-person attendance (albeit in some jurisdictions with reduced capacity), although that attendance was down significantly from pre-pandemic levels. Countless worshippers who attended regularly for their entire lives prior to the pandemic had still not set foot in a church or place of worship for close to two years. While people worried about contracting Covid from someone in the next pew or seat, many of those same folks didn't think twice about standing in line at a grocery store, navigating throngs of shoppers at Costco or eating inside a crowded restaurant. The contradictions were confusing and, for so many people today, still are.

The mixed signals and jumble of contradictory rules cast further doubt on what exactly is the prudent or acceptable way to navigate certain freedoms that we haven't fully enjoyed for a very long time. Fierce arguments in otherwise stable families have become commonplace. Sons and daughters, tired of doing nothing and determined to dance the night away with friends at a busy nightclub have become a huge source of consternation for parents who are merely trying to keep their families and elderly parents safe. Heated spouse-to-spouse arguments commonly erupt over disagreements when one partner wishes to attend a packed recreation venue or a family wedding and the other is dead-set against it. The fear that a family member could bring Covid back into the "safety sealed" home has created, and in many instances continues to create, much anxiety and even anger.

So, it's no wonder that many people still harbor fear and anxiety about the safety of doing many of the everyday things in life about which we previously never thought twice. How familiar is this thought, "I really want to go home for Thanksgiving and Christmas to finally be with my family, but I am so worried about the flight. What if I pick-up Covid or, worse yet, pass it on to my elderly parents and relatives?"

As it turned-out, the TSA reported that air travel in the few days leading up to Thanksgiving 2021 were the busiest since before the pandemic. Pent-up desire to spend time with distant family and friends boiled-over and fed that spike in travel. However, that didn't mean everyone was as eager to jump on a plane.

If you feel stuck because of the mixed signals and the lack of a definitive green flag, it is very understandable. Frankly, we all have different comfort levels in this regard and we have to be at ease with our decisions. We all have different health and risk profiles, so it's very reasonable for someone who is getting on in years and/or has serious health complications to be cautious and possibly even fearful of starting to reengage in certain activities that were previously considered ordinary. Only you know what levels of risk you feel comfortable taking, even though you may be feeling pressured by others to join in more actively than you want.

Having said this, there are a few important thoughts you may not have considered. First, once Covid is finally declassified (is no longer considered a pandemic) and regional health authorities indicate that it is safe to resume activities without restrictions, you may want to think about the actual degree of risk that remains. Nobody can assure anyone with certainty that any activity is 100% risk free and, frankly, life itself is not risk free. There is a certain degree of risk in doing just about anything and there's no doubt that people who jump in head first and live life to the fullest necessarily take on more risk than someone who does nothing. Then again, despite the added exposure to risk, the former person lives a far richer life than the latter. This is not meant to be advice and you need to make your own decisions regarding what you choose to do within your own comfort zone based on your health, your personality and other factors. But it is worth recognizing that nothing in life is risk-free.

The second important thought has to do with fear or anxiety that is merely a residual result of living through the pandemic. You may notice that you are more fearful and anxious, following this pandemic, when it comes to doing *anything*. It's one thing to have second thoughts about boarding a jet with hundreds of closely-seated passengers within a closed-air system. Nearly everyone has doubts about that, but what are the alternatives and are they any safer?

On the other hand, if you are experiencing fear of doing all sorts of regular things – things that never previously caused concern – then you may be experiencing a heightened residual impact of Covid restrictions that we all lived with for a really long time. It's likely that these anxieties will lessen and eventually resolve as you expose yourself to more of the regular activities in life. As with all of these emotional impacts of the pandemic, if your symptoms are not resolving in a reasonable timeframe – say a month or two after the pandemic is officially over – then it is time to seek some help from your family physician or mental health practitioner.

Emotional Impact #8
SOCIAL ANXIETY

As restrictions lift, life gets back to normal, and we're finally able to meet any of our friends and family in person without concern of exposure to Covid, we may find that we don't feel as socially prepared as we have been in the past. We may even feel rather inept from a social perspective! Whether we're aware of it or not, the social isolation from not being able to congregate in small or large groups for months on end took a huge toll on our social confidence. In fact, just the idea or prospect of being around and conversing with people in various in-person settings, may make you feel rather anxious. While some individuals are able to quickly shrug it off and look forward to socializing once again, others are not so keen about doing so.

A widely reported element of fallout from the pandemic is social ineptitude. After longing to meet personally in social groups, many people seem strangely unfamiliar with the norms of socializing and making conversation. It's likely that you or someone you know recently experienced a situation where a group of adults had relatively little to say to one another, having forgotten how to socialize, ask questions and tell stories. Part of what fueled this sudden social bungling was that after having been restricted from doing anything new for such a prolonged period of time, we have little that's new or interesting to talk about. Additionally, our social skills may have become rusty from underuse.

It really doesn't matter whether we're talking about your colleagues at work, social acquaintances, athletic teammates, fellow members of a club or church friends, the thought of getting back together can be a daunting thought for many. You may not even be aware of it, but perhaps you've noticed that prior to social engagements, you experience phantom pain or illness; annoying physical indicators such as nervous tics, headaches or a feeling of ill health that gets worse as the engagement grows closer. Alternatively, you may be more than aware of your fear of the upcoming meeting or event and respond to that anxiety by coming up with excuses to bail out. If you have been diagnosed with a Social Anxiety Disorder (SAD) or other anxiety disorder, it's likely that the extended isolation from Covid has exacerbated your symptoms. Consider that anxiety disorders are extremely common throughout our population and they can impact people at any age.

In the past, you may not have felt anxiety about socializing, even if you were a bit shy, but not to the extent of a full-blown disorder. However, if now you experience some social anxiety, it may only be a simple fear brought on by Covid isolation. Avoiding social engagements will not improve your fear or anxiety and may even make it worse. For most people, it's a bit like riding a bike. They say that you never really forget; after hopping on a bike for a few years, one might look at it with some initial hesitation, but once you grab the handlebar it all comes back.

Another thing that can help is to think about your upcoming event or engagement and ask yourself what you're worried about? If there are unknowns about the gathering, such as what to wear, the general plan or itinerary, who's going to be there and so-on, then learn what you can in advance. Make a strategy to help yourself have a successful and enjoyable time. If you fear that the attention will be on you and that others are studying you, relax, there's a good chance that they're just as uncomfortable as you!

You can also do a bit of 'homework' in advance, coming up with and rehearsing questions to ask certain people, based on what they were doing, dealing with or planning to do the last time you saw them. That way, you deflect attention and gain the distinct benefit of building better friendships.

After all, it was Dale Carnegie who taught us so many years ago that, ultimately, people love talking about themselves and love it even more when someone else listens.

Emotional Impact #9
BROKEN RELATIONSHIPS

What goes on behind closed doors is anyone's guess, except for the people who live there. Just because your neighbors put on a happy face when they come and go doesn't mean that things are rosy on the home front. That's why it often comes as a shock when neighbors and friends reveal that they're breaking-up. On a similar note, your relationships with family members who live in your own home may be on shaky ground; something that may have coincided with the start of the pandemic.

If you can relate to this, understand that pandemic-related relationship troubles are far more common than most people realize, because for the most part, they aren't discussed. Nonetheless, they are real and can ultimately wind-up creating much upheaval and disharmony in the household, be very costly in terms of emotional currency, and split marriages apart permanently.

It's no wonder that so many people are experiencing far more trouble in their relationships today than they were during pre-pandemic times. In many cases, the pandemic represents the proverbial straw that broke the camel's back. The relationship's foundation may have had some obscure hairline cracks to begin with, but the many stresses of the pandemic turned those cracks into worrisome fissures that could possibly result in a total collapse.

Think about it; when any member of the family is overly stressed about a challenge in his or her life; a stressor over which they have little control, everyone lives and feels it. Whether it's job loss, illness, financial difficulty or myriad other things that can go wrong in life, it often causes tension that can affect everyone; not just the person facing that difficulty. These types of things can often test marital, parent-child and sibling relationships.

Now, consider what happened during the pandemic with a view to relationships in the home. Not only did people experience those same types of stressors mentioned above, everyone in the household also had to deal with a huge strain that we've never experienced before. This pandemic is considered a once-in-a-lifetime event. We were simply not prepared; we never saw it coming and had no prior experience with it when it did arrive. Trying to cope with overwhelming uncertainty made us question everything about our lives, our jobs, our health and our world. The confidence that we previously felt about our own little world and the world around us gave assurance that, *"this is how life works."* Suddenly, we all experienced this huge epiphany that nothing is guaranteed; not even the idea that there will be toilet paper and canned food on the shelves when we go to the grocery store.

The lingering uncertainty permeated all parts of our lives. However, there was and still is, depending on where you live, the other big uncertainty; the elephant in the room. As much as we try to ignore it, there's the thought that, "I could also catch Covid and possibly even die from it." **There's no doubt that all of this stress took a toll on our relationships.**

Those little hairline cracks in our relationships may have remained hidden and unproblematic had it not been for Covid and the barrage of rubbish it brought to our lives. However, as a result of all of that emotional baggage, many of us became more impatient, moody, angry, intolerant, selfish and controlling in our relationships. Additionally, due to lockdowns, working and learning at home, and having few options for recreation and entertainment, we were at home A LOT of that time! What a perfect storm for stormy relationships.

However, it did happen and here we are; whatever negative impact the pandemic had in our relationships is a fact, so the best advice is to recognize and repair. In the next chapter, Toolbox #10 has some effective strategies to help you begin healing the hurt that Covid created in your relationship(s). Some are easy and quick to try and others will take more time and effort, but with some work, you can bring your broken relationships back to pre-pandemic status or even better!

This chapter examined a broad array of common pandemic-related impacts to people's lives and state of mind. You likely saw yourself in some or many of the scenarios. While a few helpful strategies were provided, the next chapter is chock-full of useful advice. Chapter 5 examines 10 different "toolboxes" of emotional healing, with over 50 specific things that you can do to you take control and start feeling normal in post-pandemic times.

Stephen J. Kristof

Chapter 5
Your Personal Emotional Toolboxes

You may have purchased this book because the title resonated with a nagging feeling that things just don't seem normal as you try to move into post-pandemic life. Chapter 4 was designed to clarify the reasons why you may be feeling like things just aren't right. It also presented some specific emotional stumbling blocks that you may now recognize as areas that need some attention and healing. Many of these difficulties are attributable to the Covid-19 pandemic and they're experienced by people of different cultures and demographics around the globe.

This chapter presents several "toolboxes," each containing specific tools or techniques that you can begin using to get past Covid and start feeling normal again.

Different tools apply to different people and situations; use the strategies that best relate to your individual situation. A thorough explanation of each toolbox is followed by the SUMMARY of the specific tools found in that box.

Toolbox #1
Pay Attention to Your Feelings

Understand and Accept Your Feelings. People often dismiss their own downbeat feelings as unimportant or irrelevant. In some cases, individuals ignore them, because they believe that giving validation to those ill feelings is an admission of weakness. We all have some experience with others who routinely dismiss our complaints or gloomy feelings. If you grew up with a parent who regularly dismissed your personal feelings, it probably generated significant frustration and may have even led you to avoid sharing those feelings. The same thing happens when a spouse or significant other treats us this way. Regardless of whether a dismissal of feelings is self-generated or developed as a reaction to someone who should have been more supportive, the result is the same. It leads to a person shutting down emotionally and being unwilling to express their most personal feelings.

It's very important to give validation to your feelings and, even though they may be painful or difficult, to try to understand why you feel a certain way. When people hide their negative feelings, they tend to become numb to *all* feelings; in other words, they may also develop a parallel difficulty in feeling or expressing positive and pleasurable feelings. Hiding or burying your feelings also leads people to separate from others who genuinely care about them; often replacing these supportive individuals with relationships that are dysfunctional, hurtful or even dangerous.

Accept and deal with your feelings rather than trying to distract yourself by becoming too busy to pay attention to them. The fact is that, even if you're too busy to think about what's bothering you on a conscious level, those feelings are still embedded and are not being properly addressed.

If Covid has thrown you for a loop, try to adopt the following strategies when it comes to dealing with your feelings.

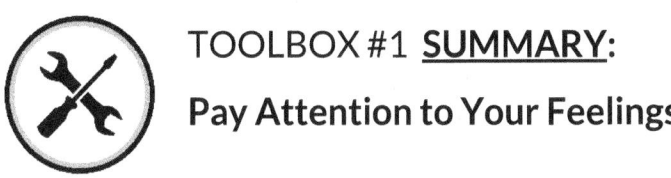

TOOLBOX #1 **SUMMARY**: Pay Attention to Your Feelings

1. Pay attention to your feelings.
They may provide a window to aspects of your life that need to change. Ask yourself what the feeling means.

2. Accept your feelings.
Validate them, because they are real. Avoid adding guilt or feeling embarrassment about your negative emotions. Your feelings don't define you; they are merely a result of experiences.

3. Try to scratch the surface of a negative emotion.
See whether it reveals people or other aspects of your life that may need further attention. For example, it's one thing to feel angry and sweep it under the rug, but an entirely different and more positive thing is to understand what's causing the anger, which can actually lead to healing.

4. Express your emotions to a truly supportive person.
If the individual tries to dismiss your feelings by saying that everyone feels that way or by trying to solve your problems in

ways that step over the line, they may care more about preserving their own power than they care about helping you.

Ideally, you're looking for an empathetic, authentic, intelligent and compassionate person who asks a lot of relevant questions and who listens intently to what you have to say.

5. Control your environment rather than trying to control your emotions.

Trying to control your emotions is a fool's game, because it's impossible to accomplish. Depending on what's causing your negative feelings, learn to accept the things that you cannot change and to change what you can.

If you are a spiritual person, try to focus on the idea that God has a plan for you and, even though you may not be able to understand why things have turned out the way they are, this is part of living in faith. Okay, it's a bit cliché, but much like in the Carrie Underwood song, "Jesus Take the Wheel", sometimes the very best thing we can do is to accept how we feel about bad situations and let God take care of the next steps. This doesn't give one Carte Blanche to give-up and purposely mess-up, but there are times in life when we've tried everything possible to control our environment and have landed on the losing side. Sometimes, *"letting go and letting God"* is the answer.

6. Strengthen your coping skills.

Many people have very weak coping skills and tend to crumble when faced with the most minor obstacle or negative circumstance. Unfortunately, unlike certain aptitudes, humans are not born with coping skills; rather, the ability to cope is developed through role modeling *(for instance a parent modeling positive coping techniques to a child)* and through practice.

In some cases, people develop practices that they think are helping to cope with stress and negative situations, but that actually make things worse. Using alcohol to deal with stress and to erase the stressor, for example, does not solve the problem, but can introduce new, more concerning problems. Instead, doing things like journaling, reframing problems as challenges to overcome, avoiding over-thinking or ruminating on the negative, creative expression, prayer and starting a positive and new project are all good ways to cope.

Toolbox #2
Treat Your Body Well

At the beginning of Chapter 4, there was a lengthy section on Covid's impact on sleep. As discussed, there are many reasons why this virus has caused insomnia, sleeplessness and poor sleep for countless people. There are some simple steps you can follow if your sleep has been negatively impacted by Covid or any other factor.

Although the pandemic has had negative impacts on some people's sleep, it has actually improved sleep for others.

However, for those whose sleep was disturbed, the stress of the pandemic, accompanied by related factors such as financial worries and other anxieties may have created sleep problems.

It is easier to distract one's self during the day, but far more difficult to do so in the quiet hours when we should be sleeping. Altered schedules that occurred due to the pandemic impacted people's biological clock; the circadian rhythm that was discussed early in Chapter 4 of this book.

In terms of helping to regain a good night's sleep, adding structure to one's day can be very helpful. Additionally, when we can't fall asleep or wake in the middle of the night and have difficulty falling back to sleep, trying to will one's self back to sleep may lead to much frustration and is far less effective than simply trying to rest. If you can't reconcile the idea of just getting some rest and this ends up causing you stress, it may be worthwhile in such instances to so some busy-work that isn't particularly stressful or mindful.

The Mayo Clinic recommends techniques such as removing visible clocks from the bedroom, avoiding daytime napping, getting regular exercise, waking each day at a regular time without sleeping in, making the bedroom more conducive to sleep and developing relaxing bedtime routines.[xxi]

In terms of treating your body well, there are other things beyond getting healthful sleep that can help us deal with the emotional fallout caused by the pandemic. Regular exercise is far more important for mood than most people realize. If the pandemic made a mess of your gym or exercise schedule, make it a priority to get your body moving again. If you routinely enjoyed regular visits to the gym or attended other fitness routines such as swimming/aqua fitness/ai chi, Zumba, tai chi, yoga, paddleboard, Pilates, or any other type of exercise, jump back in as soon as local regulations permit and safety concerns are satisfied. Medical and recreation experts tend to focus on the importance of regular exercise for our physical bodies, while underplaying the tremendous positive impact it has on our emotional and mental health.

 Another positive physical adjustment that can help us heal emotionally from the ravages of the pandemic is to reduce alcohol and caffeine intake. As a means to counter stress and boredom, many people began routinely drinking an excessive amount of alcohol; ironically, it usually has the opposite effect. If you do an internet image search using a phrase like "covid wine alcohol meme", the results, while quite amusing, reveal the extent to which ordinary people increased their alcohol consumption during Covid's uninvited presence. If your alcohol or recreational substance intake increased in response to the pandemic and now continues to be part of your routine, it would be very beneficial for your body and for your psychological state to reduce it. In a similar way, many people increased their caffeine intake, because they were tired during the day due to poor sleep the previous night. However, the extra coffees create a vicious cycle in which over-stimulation from excessive caffeine contributes to a poor sleep pattern, which in turn, creates the urge for more caffeine to stay awake during daylight hours…and it continues.

Food is another physical factor with a strong mind-body connection. In addition to sleep and exercise, our diet also has a tremendous impact on our health. It's like the old cliché, "You are what you eat." Amusingly, job search resumes that list "interests" often include cooking as a common interest. It's amusing, because we all have to eat and most of us can't afford to pay for restaurant food on a continuous basis. Why wouldn't cooking be a common interest? *That is, unless you have a spouse or loved one who happens to be an excellent cook and who you somehow sweet-talked into cooking for you on a regular basis (in which case you are a very lucky duck)!*

As widely covered in various media reports, while some people improved their eating habits immensely during the pandemic, others adopted very unhealthy diets. Shortly into the pandemic, many people who never even dared to *look* at a stove, decided to try their hand at cooking. The novelty was exhilarating, but as the months went by, many of those same newbie chefs lost their interest in making bread from scratch and experimenting with culinary masterpieces. Unfortunately, the kitchen became a lonely place again and diets regressed into greasy, salty fast food and similarly unhealthy pre-packaged, processed food.

Fewer people were actually inspired by the extra free time offered by the pandemic and made a serious commitment to improving their eating habits. Many of them have honored that commitment. For others, though, it didn't last very long.

To recap, here's a summary of the individual tools found in Toolbox #2; here's what you should be doing for your body in order to elevate your pandemic-fatigued emotional self:

TOOLBOX #2 **SUMMARY**:
Treat Your Body Well

1. Improve your sleep pattern.
Go to bed at a regular time, settling into a calm routine beforehand. Wake at the same time each day and avoid sleeping in. It's okay to give yourself a maximum of one or two free days to sleep in if you need that incentive. However, make sure that your free day(s) is consistent from week-to-week, so that you avoid slipping into a pattern in which you oversleep whenever you feel tired or your schedule permits it. When that happens, free days and regular days have no real meaning. Avoid daytime naps and add structure to your day.

Reduce caffeine intake if it is interfering with your sleep and get more physical exercise when you are awake. If you are relying on alcohol or drugs to help you sleep, be aware that alcohol before bed can often interrupt deep sleep, resulting in one feeling spent and tired despite sleeping for an adequate amount of time. Some drugs can have the same effect. If you are taking a physician-prescribed pharmaceutical to help you sleep, follow your physician's recommendations and if you wish to wean yourself off of such drugs, again, talk with your doctor.

If you can't fall asleep or have difficulty getting back to sleep after waking in the middle of the night, avoid focusing on *trying to sleep* and think, instead, about *getting some rest*. Don't sweat it if you are not actually sleeping, because even resting your body and brain can be beneficial. The key here is that if you start worrying about not falling asleep or not getting enough sleep, it's unlikely that sleep will occur. Just relax! Meditate on pleasant memories or things for which you're thankful and let your body enjoy some down time.

2. Pay attention to what's going into your body.

Be better to your physical body and your brain will thank you. Cook for yourself, being creative and resourceful. Choose fresh and whole foods to build a meal, rather than relying on processed foods that have multiple ingredients and loads of sodium (salt) and additives. If you have trouble pronouncing the ingredients listed on a food container, it's probably better to avoid putting it into your body.

Have fun with your cooking, mix it up so you're not always eating the same thing and pay attention to your major food groups. Keep your diet balanced and healthy. In general, moderation is the key, depending on your own dietary restrictions (if you have them). In our present culture, ingredients like carbs, meats and fats have been vilified. In terms of the aforementioned moderation, too much of anything is not good for you! Water can be lethal if someone drinks too much of it at once. Think about balance when you plan your meals. While most people do not need to avoid these ingredients, some people with certain medical concerns may need to stay clear of one or more of these things. Ask yourself what your familial ancestors ate and how long they lived on average. Instead of going to extremes and cutting-out certain ingredients that are unpopular at one time or another, focus more on getting fresh vegetables, fruits, fiber, wild-caught seafood and ancient whole grains into your diet.

Keep an eye on your intake of alcohol and be honest with yourself in evaluating if it is creating any level of dependency. The same goes for anything else that you are putting into your body that can create dependency or addiction. If you smoke, that's your choice, but you are making a grave choice.

When it comes to the body-mind connection, always remember that only a fool tries to fool the mind into feeling good while cheating on what he or she puts into their body. The body knows and the brain feels it too.

3. Move that body.
Regular exercise is key to physical and mental health. Do not discount the importance of physical movement and exercise when it comes to your emotional state! If you were very active before the pandemic struck, safely get back to where you were. If the concept of exercise is foreign to you, begin slowly after consulting with your physician.

Water based exercise such as swimming, aqua fitness and ai chi can be wonderfully freeing for those with limited movement. Other group fitness activities such as yoga, Pilates, tai chi, Zumba and qigong are excellent ways to move your body in non-threatening and often socially fun environments. Just walking for a half hour a day can have a far greater benefit than most people realize. When you walk in open-air settings with abundant natural scenery, such as nature parks, beaches and public gardens, the positive impact on the mind is even more potent. Of course, for the more conditioned and competitive among us, returning to more rigorous recreation and sports like tennis, hockey, curling, winter sports and ball sports in general, also elevates one's emotional state.

Toolbox #3
Reduce Screen Time and Avoid Certain Media

One of the most important changes brought about by the pandemic was that many of the in-person social things that we normally enjoyed – even thrived on – were replaced by artificial, digital meetings on remote screens. Some of that won't change a whole lot, even when the pandemic is safely behind us. For example, businesspersons who previously travelled frequently around the country or the world to conduct sales and other such meetings now meet remotely far more often than they do in-person. The exorbitant cost of travel and related expenses simply can't be reconciled when corporations compare the bang for the buck between long distance in-person meetings and those done remotely through digital technology.

The bottom line always wins in the corporate world, but that doesn't mean remote digital meetings feel as 'normal' as the real thing. In the short term, they may save money, but they may also be less effective at closing sales or fostering long-term relationships. Anyone who has travelled for business regularly understands that there are many nuances that simply cannot be replicated on a screen. Between different cultures, on screen meetings can quickly become awkward, disjointed and artificial, with gaps of extremely uncomfortable silence punctuating confused body language and facial expressions. That doesn't even scratch the surface of the depth of connection, enhanced rapport and **trust** that can develop after the in-person meeting, when executives often share conversation over dinner which is far less impersonal and more casual.

The popularity of remote digital business meetings started growing well before the pandemic, but the pandemic hastened their use due to physical and travel restrictions. What does this mean in terms of post-pandemic normality? The pandemic has increased our reliance on screens to do far more things than we ever did in the past. It's also not a very healthy trend, both in terms of our physical and our emotional well-being. What are you doing on a screen that you can do better in person? What can you change to restore your feeling of normality?

We've been itching to get out and experience life, so one of the first and most important tools in this toolbox is to get out, get off the screen and live REAL life again! After having been glued to screens for so long during the pandemic, it's so invigorating for our emotional state to shut those screens and experience real life through our eyes and the rest of our natural senses.

Several of the following tools in this toolbox are related to our use of the news media. It's not that "the news media" is inherently bad for us or that they all present a harmful view of society. On the contrary, the news media, in general, fulfill a very important and necessary role in our society, in terms of informing, explaining, educating and exposing information that might otherwise not reach you. However, it's worth considering that we have control over where we get our news and how we use it, and that can make a big difference in our mental health.

There's nothing wrong with being informed and educated in terms of what's going on in our communities, nation and world. In fact, it's considered an important part of being an informed citizen, which is one of the responsibilities of living in a free and democratic society. People who avoid news on current events often have less to talk about in social gatherings and may appear somewhat ill-informed. On the other hand, if you find that watching, reading and/or listening to news is upsetting or makes you nervous, it's probably a better idea to remove it from your diet – at least for a while – and find other things to talk about.

Indulge me for a moment and think about your answer to the question, *"Why do the media exist?"* As a former professional media educator, I would often ask new students this question. Interestingly, the most common answer was that, *"The media exist to inform and entertain us."* Guess what? Turns-out that answer is false, with the exception of non-profit public TV and radio (such as NPR and PBS in the U.S., CBC in Canada and BBC in the U.K.).

In free societies with open-market economies, the media exist, as do all businesses and corporate entities, to maximize profit. The <u>way they make that profit</u> is by producing or buying content and disseminating that content. Don't confuse how a business makes money with why it exists. Next question – how do media companies (including big media as well as bloggers and podcasters) make money? The answer is through advertising and, in some cases, subscription. In the case of advertising revenue, one equation always applies; <u>the larger the audience, the greater the advertising revenue</u>. In the case of subscription revenue; the more interesting and sensational the content, the more people subscribe.

<u>Understand that the more news media you consume, the more upset you will become</u>. I know that sounds like a gross overstatement, but consider the reasoning before you dismiss it entirely. It's in the best interest of a news media business to shape and package news stories in a way that will be as shocking, dreadful, scandalous and upsetting as possible, in order to increase audience share. It's awfully hard to look away from a terrible accident when you drive by one. It's equally difficult to change the channel or media stream when something equally terrible is about to be revealed. As mentioned, the media business is ultimately about making a profit, just as with any

business. How they make that profit is less important than the profit itself. For example, if a type of media programming were banned by legislation, the business would simply find and manufacture other content to take its place and move on. Having worked with individual reporters, producers, anchors and tech support staff, I can attest to the fact that most of them are genuinely concerned about tenets, such as journalistic integrity, objectivity, truth and quality of production. They also care about their lineup, in terms of relevance to the viewer. Well, at least the good ones care about this stuff.

However, the higher one goes up the food chain, the more likely it is that these tenets of news production become less important than how well the programming was received by the audience. Periodic ratings are always important for media production and on-air staff, because they are concerned about holding on to their jobs; it's a fear thing. Those same ratings are also important for the executives, but for entirely different reasons. They are more likely to connect ratings with dollar signs.

If you truly want to heal from the lingering emotional wounds caused by this whole Covid experience, here are some practical things you can do in terms of news media. Avoid watching 24-hour news channels exclusively. Although they are omnipresent, nobody should watch them 24/7. While these types of channels are great at delivering a non-stop stream of information, understand that much of it is tremendously repetitive and only a small fraction of what is covered during a 24-hour period is genuinely new. It's kind of like trying to rehash the same topics over and over again by changing the headlines slightly each time and interviewing different people who really don't have anything new or different to say. If you're already in a worried state about the topic, none of this is going to help, but it will intensify your overall anxiety and the feeling that things are not normal.

Along this line, if you are experiencing heightened anxiety, turn away from the swirling graphics on screens that read,

"Breaking News" or the like. This can be a trigger, spiking anxiety in PTSD and anxiety-prone individuals.

The next concept about reducing screen time is related to what happens to your body and brain as you replace real human experience in different authentic environments, with spurious experience that happens on a screen in a single dimension. There's a reason that we tell our own kids or our relatives' children to, "Get off the screen, go outside and be with friends." Have we forgotten that reason? It seems that many of us have, because while we may still counsel our younger children and relatives to do this, many of us aren't practicing what we preach! If you want to feel more normal, live more of your life off of and away from screens as much as you can.

Other media-related advice includes taking a break from social media in general. As discussed in Chapter 3, social media sources don't have the traditional gatekeepers; they don't follow and don't have to follow standards of objectivity, journalistic practices and the basic idea of truth. As a result, they can paint a picture of events, society and the world that is very skewed from reality and that is very unhealthy to consume!

Avoid any social media or other media sources (including online "experts") that focus on conspiracy theories, are clearly biased rather than balanced or that espouse hatred, suspicion and fear. In short, if a media source contributes to your feelings of anger, hate, fear, anxiety, helplessness, hopelessness, frustration, resentfulness or worthlessness, put it on your own personal "do not consume" list; banish it from your media diet!

Reinforcement theory is based on true behavioral science; the psychological impact of repetitive negative messages becomes reality. Media Effect Psychological Whiplash occurs when, just as we take one step forward and start feeling better, bad news pushes us backward two steps. The good news is that we are in control and can reduce the impact of these mechanisms by simply turning our heads away from the cacophony.

To summarize, try to follow these steps regarding your use of media to reduce lingering anxiety after the Covid pandemic.

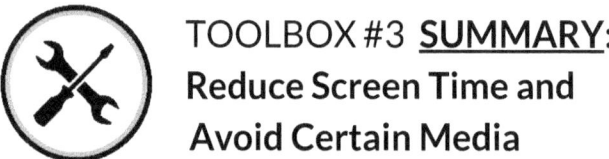

TOOLBOX #3 <u>SUMMARY</u>: Reduce Screen Time and Avoid Certain Media

1. Replace screen time with an in-person option when communicating with others.
Covid has increased the importance and prevalence of screens and monitors for communication. Don't make it worse. If you developed the unhealthy habit of turning to the screen more than you did during your pre-pandemic life, it's time to wean yourself off the screen and to start living real life.

When faced with the option of communicating with someone through a video app or actually getting together in person, choose the latter option! There will always be an element of the unreal with screen communication, so feeling normal again is facilitated by less, not more screen time.

2. Reduce consumption of 24/7 news sources.
Round-the-clock types of news channels can only maintain that kind of schedule of broadcasting all day and night by repeating the same stories, topics and messages in slightly different ways. Since the most profitable news is not positive, you're getting multiple doses of the same negative news. Reinforcement creates anxiety through the subconscious belief that the world has been sucked into a never-ending vortex of frightening and hopeless events.

3. Avoid "Breaking News" swirling types of graphics.
These types of animated intros almost always precede traumatic or negative news that adds to our feelings of anxiety. They can also trigger PTSD symptoms or feelings of angst.

4. Understand that news media (and all corporate entities) exist to maximize profit.
Accordingly, they will almost always focus on the negative and the shocking in order to get the largest audience, which results in the largest profit. How do you fit into their strategy? The impact on your emotional state as a result of watching an ongoing stream of reinforced shock and awe matters less to media executives than does the fact that you and as many others as possible are watching.

5. In general, turn off the screens if and when you can.
It's not just the news media that contribute to the feeling of abnormality. If you are an adult with children, grandchildren, nieces or nephews, how often have you urged them to get off the screen, and get out there and play with friends? We have all said it and some of us still say it. Why? Because we realize how much more important it is for the child's social and physical development to do something other than staring at a screen like a zombie.

Practice what you preach and endeavor to reduce your own screen time for the very same reasons. There's nothing wrong with watching TV, being entertained and engaged through social media, playing video games and just surfing the internet, but these activities can be overdone. When they, collectively, start taking up more and more of your waking hours, remember that none of them will heal your mind as much as living real life away from screens.

6. Disconnect from any social media, online news or other media source that leaves you feeling angry, fearful, agitated, frustrated, hateful, resentful or that attacks your feelings of self-worth.

Similarly, don't walk, but RUN away from any media stream that encourages hatred, espouses obvious lies or untruths and/or focuses on bizarre conspiracies.

Toolbox #4
Focus on the Positive

How many times can you remember someone – anyone – telling you to, "Focus on the positive"? Everyone has heard the advice and some of us hear it more than others. Whoever said it, or keeps saying it, does so with the best of intentions, but does it work at all? If you're like most people, when someone tells you to look at the positive side or, worse yet, to stop being so negative, you likely dig in your heels and become even more focused on your negative thoughts? Right? Honestly…right?

Telling someone to focus on the positive is pretty useless advice, so then why is it the title of this section? Quite simply, because it is not someone else's advice; rather, it can become your own mantra and you will likely be taken aback at how easy it is to do and how effectively it can change your mood. As encouraging as it sounds, you need to know *how* to think more positively.

First of all, you need to be conscious of times when you suddenly feel angry, impatient, worried, frustrated, short-tempered or discouraged. For garden-variety situations where one can easily self-identify that they have become overly negative because of the pandemic, or where it's obvious to them why they feel a certain way, it's important to mentally establish that connection. If the connection isn't so obvious, don't try to self-psychoanalyze; in trying to figure out what's making you feel a certain way, you may be woefully wrong about it and cause even greater problems for yourself. *(If your negative mood or feelings are so significant that they are disabling and you have no idea why you feel these ways, actual psychoanalysis by a professional, may offer much clarity and tools for healing.)*

Being lucid about your negative feelings and their origins can be very helpful. Even if you're not certain why you feel a certain way, simply having awareness of your feelings can allow you to *choose* to change your thought pattern. **Be willing to change.** This is tremendously important! Once you become aware of the extent to which you have negative thoughts, it allows you to understand that change is vital and necessary. Get beyond the teenage stage. When you were in high school, remember how you sometimes grumbled that you had to do homework, study for tests and complete projects to please your teacher? Even though your teacher may have told you that you were really doing the work for your own future, for yourself, and not for them, it may have been hard to believe at that point in your life. If you have become mired in negative thinking, understand that changing it will, ultimately, improve your own happiness and enjoyment of the gift of life. Remember, you are in charge here!

Fortunately, there are many practical techniques in the toolbox of positive thinking that you can try out with relatively little planning or effort. One of the most effective is to focus on gratitude. Rather than grumbling about how this or that isn't going your way or how the pandemic has interfered with your life, make a very conscious effort to remember and think about all of the ways in which you have been blessed or consider yourself fortunate. Some counselors recommend that their patients keep a "**Gratitude Journal**" as an effective way to become more consciously aware of the many different things – big and small – for which they should be thankful. When using the journaling technique, it doesn't take long for one to realize that the blessings far outweigh the complaints. It only takes about five minutes a day to record your thoughts about the good things in one's life and it's very well worth the effort.

If the idea of starting a gratitude journal sounds intriguing, but you have no idea where to start, there are literally thousands of printed versions for sale online, at booksellers and at specialty shops; you don't need to look very hard to find one. Most of them offer the advantage of a guided journey into the practice of gratitude journaling, while others simply have decorative headings with spaces underneath to record one's reflections. Alternatively, you can make and decorate your own fancy journal if that's more your style, or it can be nothing more than a standard composition book that you fill with your own ideas on your own terms.

Regardless of how it looks or how you approach it, the main idea is that you spend a portion of your day – preferably at the beginning or end of your day – during which you think and write about <u>specific</u> things that are good in your life.

Many people find that if they leave it to, "whatever pops into your head", the vagueness leads to writer's block and the entire exercise becomes frustrating and counterproductive. Instead, it's really helpful to compartmentalize your areas of gratitude, based on factors such as the following journal prompts.

Feeling Normal Again

Here are 32 specific prompts to consider when writing in your Gratitude Journal or just musing about things for which you're thankful:

- Relationships (All)
- Personal Qualities
- Things to Look Forward to
- Challenges
- Opportunities
- Where You Live
- Career (Past & Present)
- Special Talents
- Pets or Animals
- Simple Pleasures
- Finances & Assets
- People Who Help You
- Your Love Life
- People Who Support You
- Nature
- Material Possessions
- Accomplishments
- Good Memories
- Spirituality & Faith
- Education
- Your Freedoms
- Childhood
- Skills
- How You've Grown
- Your Body
- Your Home
- Health
- Weather
- Favorite Foods
- Travel
- Hobbies & Recreation
- Difficult Events, Problems or Relationships That Led to Your Growth as a Person

Now, understand that this isn't a comprehensive list of the different types of things that you can mull over for gratitude journaling, but it's a good start. By the way, did you notice that "Material Possessions" is one of the last categories listed above?

Although the other prompts are not listed in any particular order, that particular one is near the bottom on purpose. Our society places far more value on things than they are worth, in terms of what brings us true, lasting happiness.

Treat your journal as a living resource. That means that it's more than just an object. Your gratitude journal is not merely a repository of words or a book that's separate from your life. Rather, it *is* your life. Practicing journaling of any sort is also a practice in mindfulness, which is being in the moment. As such, strive to integrate your daily reflections of gratitude into the next 24 hours of life. Continue to reflect on what you wrote. If you are a spiritual person, bring your reflections of gratitude into your prayer life, thanking God for these graces and blessings.

The advantages of cultivating gratitude are many; foremost among them being that you replace the negative thoughts with positive ones. In doing so, you program yourself to increasingly be aware of, seek out and think about the positive, which can have surprisingly positive implications on your physical and mental health, relationships, peacefulness, sleep, self-esteem, hope and, of course, happiness.

In a similar vein to gratitude journaling, consider that reinforcement theory is not merely about exposure to media messages. **People program themselves all of the time by simply reinforcing certain thoughts and patterns of thought**. Our inner self-talk and our outward messages to others become our own reality, regardless of how much we may not initially even believe what we are saying or how outlandish it sounds. For example, a student who repeatedly thinks, "I'm awful at math. I'm going to fail all of my tests this semester and will ultimately fail this math course," will ultimately fail most, if not all, of those math tests and will not earn the credit. Of course, for that student, math may have not been a forte, but that weakness need not have led to failure. Understanding that something is a weakness and focusing on how to strengthen it is far different from giving-up and accepting failure in advance of even trying.

What about the student who actually is really good at a subject, but who struggles with tests? In many cases, the problem isn't in understanding the material, but rather, lies in a deep-seated *belief* that one will fail the test. Of course, when that self-fulfilling prophecy comes true and the student fails that test despite the fact that they studied very hard and knew the material exceptionally well, the false belief gains traction. With continued reinforcement through negative self-talk, that student is eventually convinced that they will fail any test. This reinforced thought becomes truth, even though it was not at all accurate.

The same philosophy applies to all manner of life situations and challenges. If you are feeling like the pandemic has sucked the "normal" out of everyday living and thinking, part of it may be due to your own reinforcement of negative thoughts regarding how life is not yet normal and may never feel normal again. Continue to focus on the negative and this will become your own "new normal". The simple solution is to change the way you think; focus on the positive. Focusing on and reinforcing the positive becomes your reality; you also attract positive energy instead of negative energy, which means that better things will come your way.

Another technique that can help you avoid dwelling on the negative and focusing, instead, on the positive is to **turn on some filters**. If you've ever searched for a product through online shopping, you'll recall that most store sites provide a series of filters on the left side of your screen, allowing you to checkmark specific sub-categories that you're looking for, as well as to exclude things that you're not interested in. Perhaps you're looking for a new dishwasher and the available filters are for brand, size, decibel level, front vs. top controls and other considerations. As you check the filters, the results are custom tailored to fit your needs and desires.

Well, have you ever considered checking some filter boxes for your own life? If you realize that you tend to dwell on the negative and it's affecting your ability to bounce back, mentally, from the pandemic, then establish some new filters. Avoid spending time with pessimistic people who only bring you down or, worse yet, put you down. Run away from toxic people if you're able to do so. If you cannot get away from these types of individuals because you work with them, live with them or have some other necessary connection to them, don't make enemies of them (that's not going to accomplish anything positive for you; quite the opposite – you'll just make things much more stressful for yourself), but by the same token, put your guard up and don't let them get to you. Spend as little time with these toxic people as possible.

Choose to spend time, instead, with positive people who support you and put you in a good mood. You know who they are; people who are always optimistic, filled with joy and who always try to find the silver lining. If you are surrounded by negative or toxic people at work and at home, you may have to cultivate some positive new friendships. Find a new volunteer gig that makes you feel good, or a sport or club that places strong value on socializing. You're sure to find people who like to laugh, enjoy your company, are supportive and who seem to really enjoy life. Filter those types of people *into* your life!

Filter out other negative influences such as TV and movies, video games and other entertainment streams that glorify violence and death, that dwell on poor choices, and that make bizarre and anti-social behaviors seem normal. Instead, filter *in* content that makes you feel good about yourself and about the world around you. Read books by inspirational authors, watch videos and Ted Talks by motivational speakers, watch uplifting movies and try to find the humor in life. Choose to laugh instead of cry and, when you need to cry, express the hurt to someone who loves and encourages you.

Yet another simple positive thinking technique that can yield much benefit is in **daring to dream again**. One thing that the pandemic was exceptionally good at was in dashing our dreams. Many people were knocked backward and knocked down in different ways due to the scourge that was Covid-19. On a global basis, vast numbers of people – certainly into the hundreds of millions – lost their jobs, homes, retirement savings and/or various opportunities due to the pandemic. For some, the pandemic swept away dreams of a bigger or nicer home (or the prospect of even owning a home), while for others, it put the brakes on a post-secondary educational pathway to a brighter future. While some struggled with the loss of vacations and luxurious options to spend their leisure time, others struggled far more with the loss of income and future career growth. Whether it was trivial or truly life-altering, Covid shattered a lot of dreams. A lot of people are stuck in a depressed mode of thinking when it comes to dreaming again, even though many circumstances have improved.

It is highly recommended that you begin actively re-programming yourself in this regard. Dare to dream again on a very conscious level. Replace, "I can't do this or that anymore," with, "I can't wait until I can do this or that again." Exchange, "My career is shot," or, "That boat of opportunity has sailed," with, "This is exciting - things are opening-up again. Now I can look for a new opportunity." The opportunities may not be shouting at you, but keep your eyes and ears open, because they will show up. We may not see a return of the "roaring 20's" that occurred following the combined end of World War I and the 1918 Spanish Flu pandemic, but one thing is clear and it's that people are very anxious to return to a normal life again, including a lot of spending and a celebratory mood that can kick economies and new opportunities into gear.

It might help to realize that you are not alone; in fact, you are surrounded by people of all ages who have also had their dreams squashed or at least altered due to the pandemic. They, too, will need to move ahead, just like you. You may need to do some retrofitting, some reconfiguration of yourself or your plans, or you may need to reinvent yourself to a certain degree, but regardless, your dreams *are* attainable! It's a lot easier to give-up and blame your lost dreams on the pandemic than it is to chin-up and put your nose to the grindstone. In the end, only you will regret not getting back up and trying to reach your goals – whatever they are.

Some people don't let circumstances like bad luck, unexpected crises or even advanced age get in the way of their dreams. Harry Bernstein, who worked as a magazine editor and script reader until he retired at 62, didn't give up on his dream to be a published author. He wrote his first of four books in 2007 when he was 93; that book was published when he was 96 years old. Then there was Gladys Burrill who, in 2004, completed her first marathon…at the age of 84! Eight years later, she completed the 26.2-mile Honolulu Marathon at the age of 92. And just about everyone knows who Susan Boyle is. Despite being mocked and jeered for years, Susan gathered the courage to audition for Britain's Got Talent when she was 47. It led to success beyond her wildest dreams; seven albums and countless performances later, it's rumored that she's now worth $40 million.

Determination is far more powerful than a pandemic that may have knocked you back a few steps. In short, don't allow the pandemic to take the blame for your unfulfilled dreams. It really is up to you.

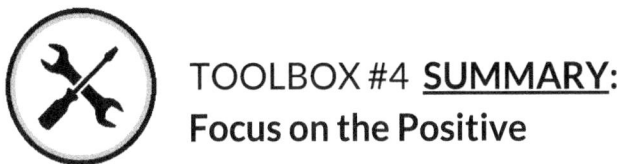# TOOLBOX #4 **SUMMARY**: Focus on the Positive

1. Be aware of your negative feelings and be open to change.
Do you have an idea of how often negative ideas are part of your thought process? We've been bombarded with negative ideas throughout the pandemic and many of us have modeled that into our own way of thinking. You are in charge of this change; you are only doing it for yourself and not for anyone else! Choose to consciously replace your chronically negative thoughts with positive ones.

2. Start a Gratitude Journal.
Take 5 minutes a day and write about the things you're thankful for. Think about the blessings and aspects of your life for which you realize you're fortunate. It's an extremely effective way of focusing on the positive and can impact your life in many ways, including increasing happiness, reducing anxiety, improving self-esteem and more. In the preceding description of this toolbox, there are 31 areas to consider when thinking about gratitude; using a guided process for this type of journaling makes it an enjoyable and far easier process! To cultivate an ongoing mindfulness of gratitude, it is recommended that you consciously think about each day's journal entry for the next 24 hours.

3. Program Yourself to Be Positive!

Reinforcement Theory, which has been discussed often in this book, is a very real process in which people are programmed to believe and think in a desired way using a repetitive process. Media and other people can use this quite successfully on us, but we can also use it on ourselves with even greater effectiveness. Another term for this is "Self-Fulfilling Prophesy". In short, we believe what we tell ourselves. Our "self-talk" and our messages to others permeate our thought process and what we say becomes our reality.

If you've allowed yourself to dwell on negative thoughts about your weaknesses, inabilities, undesirable outcomes, losses, failures and such, it becomes extremely difficult to feel encouragement or to consider that any positive will come your way. Make a conscious effort, instead, to dwell on the positive.

4. Turn on Some Filters.

It's common to use filters when shopping for something online; why not use filters in our own lives? Filter out the negative, the discouraging and the hurtful influences in your life. If you can avoid them, filter out toxic people who leave you feeling sapped and doubtful. Filter out those who belittle you and attack your self-esteem.

Choose, instead, to fill your life with people who are optimistic, supportive and joyful. If you can't get away from the negative and toxic people, join a new club, team or volunteer situation and expand your social circle with positive people. Filter out the TV series, movies, video games and other entertainment content that glorifies or focuses on violence and anti-social behavior. Select other content and entertainment that is wholesome and hopeful! Choose to surround yourself with things and activities that make you happy.

5. Dare to Dream Again.

Covid effectively shut down the hopes and dreams of so many people. We've been sucked down a vortex of negativity that unfortunately make it seem like many of our dreams are not unattainable. Whether the dreams relate to career, education, finances, relationships or special projects and achievements, you need to realize that the world is *still* your oyster. Yes, you are a few years older, but you are the only obstacle at this point, in your drive toward that dream! Don't blame the pandemic for your own lack of drive and determination to achieve your dreams.

6. Renew Your Relationships.

The pandemic made a mess of many people's relationships at home, work and even in our spiritual lives. It's very difficult to remain positive when our relationships are in disrepair. Focus on how you've changed and take the steps to change what *you* can to bring your relationships back to where they were prior to the pandemic and even better. If you practiced a religion and attended worship regularly before the pandemic, returning to worship will also have a profound impact on your ability to think positively.

Toolbox #5
Take Control of Your Anxiety

Do you realize that everyone feels anxious? That's right, every single person experiences anxiety in their lives. Now, that doesn't mean that everyone feels anxious to the same extent or with the same frequency, but it is a feeling that everyone can at least relate to at some level. Living through almost two years of heightened stress, frustration, social isolation and negativity impacted everyone's overall feelings of anxiety; for those who were already prone to feeling anxious, the impact was obviously worse. It's important to differentiate between anxiety and anxiety disorder. At some point in anyone's life, we experience anxiety that is usually associated with stressful experiences or upcoming events. Attending a job interview, for example, is an experience that will generate quite a bit of anxiety for most people. First dates, waiting for results from health tests, delivering a speech in front of a crowd, buying a new home; these are things that often generate anxiety. However, when the anxiety is persistent and the episodes last longer than the situation that led to the anxious feeling, a disorder may be at play. The big difference between the two is that regular anxiety is something that will go away on its own, while an anxiety disorder may not.

About 18% of the US population – about 40 million people – live with a form of anxiety disorder. Yes, it's that common. Feelings of fear, worry and terror, sometimes intense, along with physical manifestations such as rapid heartbeat, panic attacks and even gastrointestinal symptoms can sometimes accompany anxiety disorders. They can also interfere with daily functions and lead to avoidance of activities, places and situations that could be important and even enjoyable. The techniques for dealing with anxiety in this particular toolbox can effectively reduce anxiety, but in cases where the symptoms are more acute as described above, a professional mental health assessment followed by treatment and management of the disorder is vital. Keep in mind that anxiety can have genetic and even physical origins, so proper diagnosis is an important first step. Factors such as common medications and even diet can increase anxiety in some people, so getting qualified help can be a crucial step.

Regardless of origin, the following practices can help to reduce the intensity and frequency of anxiety. Popular external tools to control anxiety involve things like diet, exercise, square breathing, massaging your hands and bringing order to a messy surrounding. However, the most effective strategies for controlling anxiety involve doing it from *the inside-out*. The first of these relates to the widespread practice of habitual anxiety. Some mental health practitioners believe that for many people, anxiety has a habitual root. Anxiety can also result from distorted thinking about various situations. When this is the case, one can greatly reduce anxiety by understanding its role in how one mentally deals with those situations. Remember that reinforced thoughts, regardless of how false or outlandish they may be, become truth and reality. So how does this relate to anxiety? **Chronic worrying reinforces the idea that worrying works.** It's a simple relationship that's explained by the *false alarm theory*. Despite our constant worrying about bad outcomes, those bad things only occur about 10% of the time. In fact, in a third of the cases in which an outcome is bad, it's usually better than expected. This is worth repeating; <u>things go our way most of the time and when they don't, they're often not that bad</u>. Those are not bad odds, in fact, they're great odds! If a seasoned gambler knew that the odds would be in their favor 90% of the time, they would be making a lot more bets with a lot more money.

Let's apply this to your anxiety; here's how it works. ***Each time we precede an outcome by worrying about it and the outcome turns out to be good, over time, our subconscious mind becomes convinced that worrying was responsible for the good outcome.*** It becomes a habit that reinforces the false relationship. In other words, our worrying, fear and nervousness had nothing at all to do with the positive outcome, but multiple episodes of this cycle imprint the idea that "worry = good outcome". As we repeat this cycle, we feed the same subliminal message and it becomes a reality that guides our future responses to stressful situations and unknown outcomes. Our thought process and expectations about potentially awful outcomes – and even ones that are only minor but unwanted – become distorted as a matter of habit and routine.

This process of subconsciously programming ourselves to accept that worrying is somehow responsible for a good outcome is very common, yet the average person has no idea that it's a big part of why they frequently feel anxious. It also has a subtly insidious side; in the event that we catch ourselves feeling calm and at peace while awaiting an unknown and potentially bad outcome, we feel that *not worrying about it* will somehow mystically make the bad thing happen; of course, anxiety follows. Now that you have this knowledge, you can use it as an extremely effective tool to consciously reduce anxiety when you are facing a potentially troublesome outcome.

There is one caution, though, about this particular tool of which you need to be aware. Just because you now realize that there is no real connection or truth to "worry=good outcome" thinking, please don't make the inference that you need not prepare for situations where preparation is key to a good outcome or success!

A 23-year-old man had been working in his first entry-level career job for a few years, when a more responsible position opened-up at a different location in that same corporation; the new role would be a logical next-step in his climb up the ladder. He applied for the position and, due to his qualifications and a glowing recommendation from his local manager, got an interview.

He sought to prepare himself by borrowing from a local co-worker in that same position, several thick binders containing protocols and other important information; a gold mine of preparation that would give that young man a distinct advantage in getting that job. When he opened the first binder, he felt a rush of adrenaline that quickly turned into worry, heart palpitations and fright! The young man convinced himself that reading and studying the information would cause him to become even more anxious; an anxiety that he believed would carry through to the interview and surely disqualify him from getting the job.

He migrated his twisted logic to a bold position that sounded something like, "I'm not going to prepare at all. If I'm the right person for the job, they will know it. After all, they are hiring a person, not binders of information or rehearsed interview responses."

Little did he expect when he walked through the door that he would be directed to sit at the head of a long conference table with eight people surrounding him and asking questions… questions that, of course, could have easily been answered from the information in those binders. The interview was painfully embarrassing for the young man and, likely, for the managers interviewing him as well. You can guess what the outcome was. By the way, that young man was the author of this book. Lesson learned. The point is that, although choosing to worry has nothing to do with a good outcome, choosing not to prepare when it's necessary for a good outcome is a sure way to secure a bad outcome.

In addition to breaking the false alarm anxiety cycle, there are other effective tools that can make a big difference in one's anxiety. Freedom from anxiety comes from inside-out as noted earlier. Choosing to practice calming mind exercises can be part of this overall strategy. Many mental health professionals and associations, including the Mayo Clinic, suggest a countdown approach. The idea is, when you're feeling particularly worried or anxious, divert your attention from the feeling by grounding yourself. Think about five items or objects that you can **see**, four things you can **feel**, three things you can **hear**, two things you can **smell** and one thing you can **taste**. It may sound a bit too simple to work, but it actually is quite effective!

Another internal anxiety reducing behavior is to spend some time trying to identify specific triggers that set you off. Why is your response to these triggers so disproportionate to the actual situation or thought? An awful lot of anxiety stems from specific traumatic experiences or episodes that were never properly or fully dealt with. Are you able to connect one or more anxiety triggers with an event in your past? This is hard to do on your own, but in some cases, people are more or less aware of such a connection and when that connection can be more consciously established, they can then begin to reflect on how it continues to shape current thoughts and behaviors. Sometimes we don't understand why we respond to things the way we do, but when we become aware of the reasons, it's much easier to make forward progress in our lives. The key with this tool is to understand that life is much easier and more enjoyable when we have control over our present emotions and behaviors, rather than allowing past events to control our present and future.

The final tool in the anxiety toolbox is how to control performance anxiety. For some people, the concept of "performance" is actually linked to being a performer on a stage in front of a large audience, or being a host of a live television or radio broadcast. For most of us, performance isn't so formal or fancy, but it's still part of our lives. In a sense, we perform whenever someone is watching and, potentially, judging us. A teacher or professor in front of the class, a lawyer in the courtroom, anyone at a job interview, anyone on a first date, an athlete in a crucial game, a student writing a test, a senior going for a mandatory driving test, a lover concerned about sexual performance; these are all very common types of performances that often cause people to experience much anxiety. Endless other performance-like situations for everyday people living everyday lives also come into play and, no matter how much other people may dismiss these situations as routine, they may still create worry and anxiety.

Something that works exceptionally well in combating performance anxiety is to understand the difference between adrenaline and anxiety. Prior to the performance, our adrenal gland produces the hormone adrenaline. Stemming back to our human origins, adrenaline would help our distant ancestors in a fight or flight response with respect to hunting an animal, running from a charging animal or fighting an enemy; in essence, performances. In modern times, our bodies continue to produce adrenaline in response to stressful situations or performances. However, we have lost sight of its valuable purpose and often create a misunderstood response to it. Adrenaline does raise the heart rate and may make us feel flushed along with other physical manifestations that we often misread as feeling nervous.

Rather than embracing the adrenaline as a support to help us perform better, we regard it as a bad thing which, in turn, increases our anxiety. The simple technique here is to consciously and properly decode the adrenaline effect as a useful chemical that can make us sharper, quicker and more energetic. Isn't that what we really need before any performance task?

Here's a recap of the inside-out path to controlling anxiety:

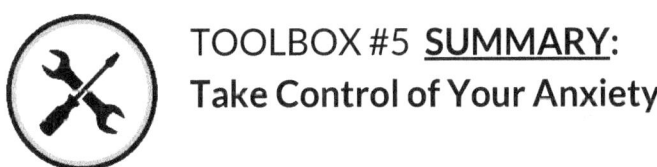

TOOLBOX #5 __SUMMARY__:
Take Control of Your Anxiety

1. Understand that worrying and anxiety do not create good outcomes!

There is no correlation whatsoever between worrying and the outcome. Regardless of our worrying, potentially bad outcomes only occur about 10% of the time and, even then, are often not as bad as we expect. If we repeatedly worry about potentially bad outcomes and 90% of the time the outcome is actually good, the pattern reinforces the false perception in our brains that worrying prevents bad things from happening. It's obviously not true, but we begin to believe it on a subconscious level.

The result is a pattern of worry and anxiety that precedes any event or situation with an uncertain outcome. Armed with this knowledge, we can reduce our anxiety greatly by focusing on this fact.

A sidebar to this tool is also understanding that when you eventually do feel calm prior to an unknown or potentially bad outcome, embrace that tranquility.

2. Practice calming grounding exercises when you feel anxious.

One method that works particularly well and quickly is to focus on five items or objects that you can see, four things you can feel, three things you can hear, two things you can smell, and one thing you can taste.

3. Identify anxiety triggers in your life and reflect on their origins.

Some people have a vague or conscious awareness that past events or traumatic experiences are connected to certain anxiety triggers. Unfortunately, when such experiences are not fully or properly processed and dealt with, they can linger and impact current feelings and behaviors. Carrying unresolved past burdens can weigh down an individual's present life and future opportunities as one continues to experience heightened anxiety.

By identifying these connections, you can start the process of healing. Look at a troubling or even traumatic past experience through a new lens and see it for what it is; something that occurred earlier in life. Do not give these types of memories permission to continue impacting your current emotions and behaviors. Plan to be in control as opposed to allowing something in the past to control who you are in the present.

4. Performance anxiety? Choose to allow adrenaline to work FOR you.

Whether you feel anxious before a formal performance or an everyday act that feels like one, use the trick that stage performers are taught as part of their formal education. Rather than trying to eliminate the useful adrenaline that our bodies produce before and while we need to 'perform', use it to your advantage. You may misinterpret as anxiety, the physical sensations of an adrenaline rush, but it is something quite different.

Adrenaline helps us to perform better; it makes us sharper, quicker and stronger. Viewing adrenaline as a negative thing will actually make you far more anxious and you probably won't perform very well either! Embrace the adrenaline and be thankful for the assistance your body is providing.

Stephen J. Kristof

Toolbox #6
Renew Friendships and Start New Ones

The widespread social isolation created by the pandemic has resulted in deep consequences in terms of life feeling abnormal. Grandparents and grandchildren were isolated from one another, people were isolated from loved ones in hospitals or nursing homes and socializing with friends was strictly off limits during successive waves of the pandemic. Weddings were postponed, many of them indefinitely, while reunions, festivals and special events were also off the table. When social restrictions were lifted and we were once again allowed to do these types of social things, a good portion of our population held off for fear of contracting one of the deadly variants. This was in spite of the fact that many of those same people were double and even triple vaccinated. Quite frankly, the scare stuck.

As discussed at greater length in Chapter 4, one of the major impacts from a post-pandemic perspective is that our social skills have been weakened. Life certainly doesn't feel normal when previously lively social butterflies would rather stick to themselves and avoid venturing out into social situations. It doesn't feel normal when we don't look forward to or even dread entertaining friends and relatives; particularly when that was something that we always really enjoyed. It also doesn't feel normal when we stumble for something to talk about and conversation that used to come so fluidly now seems stilted and awkward.

The easy way to strengthen our social competence muscle is to simply start exercising it. It may not be something you feel comfortable doing, but neither does working out at the gym after you've been absent for a few years. Let's face it; you're going to be spending a lot more time on this earth, so you might as well start trying to enjoy one of the most awesome parts of human life, which is of course, the privilege of being with others and sharing conversation with them. You could be the richest person in the world, but without the love of other people, your rich life would be very lonely and sad.

To that end, here are some things you can do to restore the social part of who you are. First, reach out to others, even if they haven't made the effort. Once you feel safe and comfortable with the idea of meeting with other people in person, whether in public settings such as restaurants and cafes, outdoors or in your own home, you need to realize that not everyone will be there yet. Reach out and call the people who you miss and from whom you've become disconnected. Start slow - get together for coffee, tea or an adult beverage if that's your style. If you previously met on a routine basis with coworkers, fellow retirees or another social group and that group has yet to reassemble, be the one who makes the first call and get it in gear again!

An important thing to consider is **who among your friends has been a genuinely supportive and positive influence on you?** The pandemic has created a convenient juncture at which you can selectively pick and choose who you wish to socialize with, based on how they've made you feel in the past. Before the pandemic, it was more difficult to suddenly stop accepting someone's invitations than it is now that some relationships have been 'temporarily' suspended. This takes a bit of reflection to understand the difference between people who may be fun to be with because they are popular, trendy and adventuresome – and – people who are truly there for you, who respect and care for you and who have your best interests at heart. Sometimes the fun of being with popular, trendy and adventuresome people fades pretty quickly once they're gone and you're feeling like less of a person. This is not to say that anyone who is popular and fun to be with is a bad influence for you; not at all! Some of those folks are the absolutely best people to hang with! It's just a point of reflection to help gauge the type of relationship you have, and what it does for your mood and your soul. Obviously, it would be foolish to rekindle a pre-pandemic relationship with someone who is toxic but fun to be with.

When you edit your list of friends, give a lot of thought to how people make you feel during and after spending time with them. You've likely gathered an eclectic pool of social friends throughout the years, from people you've met in different circumstances, such as school, work, sports, clubs and friends of friends. You may have noticed that some of these friendships have waned over the years as your interests and commonalities diverged. These people may not be very interesting to you anymore and, to be fair, you may not be all that interesting to them either. There may be others who are braggarts; people with extremely low self-esteem who often put you down and belittle you in order to validate their own false sense of importance. Some of the acquaintances on your list expect you to do all of the work, to attempt to get their attention, while treating your poorly and ignoring you. You may also have a user or two on your list; people who take and take, never give and rarely show gratitude. These people leave us feeling used, foolish and frustrated. You should waste neither the time nor the emotional effort on these people.

Make a better investment in better friends. Focus on those who are genuine, who are empathetic, who are compassionate, who like you for the person that you are. Nurture the relationships you have with those who are fun to be with, positive, cheerful and who exude positive energy.

Another tool in this toolbox is to force yourself to call instead of text. Real human conversation in which you can hear the other person, or better still, hear and see them, is vastly superior to merely texting someone. Communication theorists have long believed that words, alone, convey only 7% of the overall message in interpersonal conversation. Your non-verbal communication (such as your body language) and your paralanguage (such as your speaking tone and pace) account for a whopping 93% of the message. This explains why so many arguments and hurt feelings occur from misinterpreted texts. Everyone knows how easy it is to misinterpret the intention and emotion behind a text; even with those little emoji text pictures.

Another means of improving your post-pandemic social skills is to begin entertaining again, if that's something that you enjoyed and did frequently before Covid. Of course, not everyone is so comfortable with hosting a party, reunion or get-together. Even having another person or a couple over for coffee and pastries – a pretty simple gesture – can throw some folks for a loop and cause them much anxiety! You can always tell who the social butterflies are in your neighborhood, condo or apartment, and who the hermits are. Some folks are constantly having others over, others host only occasionally and then there are those who shut their doors to everyone except, perhaps, family. We all have different comfort levels and needs when it comes to having social, work or other friends to our homes. Certainly, as the guest list grows, the menu expands and the formality increases, so too does the amount of planning, organizing and stress. Some of us absolutely thrive on entertaining, despite all of the preparation and the overarching uncertainty of how it will go! Others, well, not so much.

This also explains why some of us had far greater difficulty getting through the social isolation of the pandemic than others. Those who prefer to be at home most of the time, who rarely meet others outside of work and never have anyone over ultimately had little change in their social lives. The party animals and extroverts among us were hit hard. Regardless of where you stand on the spectrum of voluntary socializing, one thing remains true; friends are far more important in our lives than most of us realize. They represent one of the most vital support systems in our lives. Fostering relationships with good friends and nurturing those relationships through regular contact contributes strongly to our emotional and physical health. Families are, or at least should be, the most important source of love, support, guidance, care and attention in our lives. However, we are complex beings and have lives outside of our families as well. For some, there is no family to lean on. Loneliness is one of the most painful feelings we experience, so for those people, friends are the best prescription.

Going out to restaurants and events with friends is a great way to keep your social friendships alive. Once you feel safe in our post-pandemic world, this should be high on your list. However, by hosting friends at our homes, those relationships become far closer and more supportive. Also consider that if your friends are always the ones doing the inviting and you never reciprocate, it likely leaves them feeling resentful and that's not something that cultivates strong relationships. If you have a healthy group of social friends, but avoid having anyone over, break out of that bubble and start by hosting a very simple get-together with one or two friends.

However, if you previously enjoyed entertaining guests in your home and it's been a year or longer since you've hosted a party, family celebration or social gathering, you may be in for a surprise in terms of how much more effort it seems to take. Don't forget that you're a few years older than before the pandemic started so, depending on your age, entertaining and hosting social events might take a bit more effort. Regardless of your age, some aspects of having company over, such as menu planning, cleaning the home, and preparing food and beverages, are more daunting since you haven't done them in a while. The good advice here is to start easy and casual. Avoid complicated meals if you're providing food and, if possible, order a pizza or another crowd pleaser. If you must cook, ditch the haute cuisine for now and stick with burgers and sausages! You will thank yourself after. Another option you may not have considered is to host a potluck, which is far less intimidating, because the focus is divided among everyone who attends. Catering is, yet, another alternative which allows you to focus on things other than food. Finally, emphasize to your guests that it is a very casual get-together; that way everyone, including you, feels a lot more comfortable and at ease.

When you do start meeting again with family and friends at your place, at theirs or at public places like restaurants and banquet halls, it's likely that you may find there's far less to discuss because you've all been focused on a rather singular news subject for the longest time. It would be wise to "stock the pond", so to speak, in terms of preparing some conversation points and topics in advance. Ensure that your topics have nothing to do with the pandemic or the currently divisive political theatre. As Dale Carnegie taught, people become far more engaged in conversation when they are asked questions about themselves, their lives and their opinions. Everyone wants to feel important. We love it when others ask us questions and actually listen to our answers and musings. Think about things that you don't already know about your guests, what you would like to know about them and situations that may have changed in their lives. These are good options for your "ask about" list. Listen intently to what they say and practice the good habit of asking new questions based on their answers to questions you just asked. Asking their opinion on a subject is a good idea *(as long as you avoid religion and politics),* but be ever so careful to avoid judging or disrespecting their opinions if you've asked for them. Likewise, trying to convince your guest(s) that your opinion is superior to theirs is absolutely off limits!

It may sound a bit odd to prepare conversation beforehand, but doing so will enrich the conversation that ensues! In fact, you'll find that doing a bit of "socializing homework" makes your own time with others far more enjoyable than it ever was, because it motivates your company to perk-up and become more engaging.

Yet another tool that can be of immeasurable help in the realm of social isolation is that of putting yourself out there to help others. We volunteer, of course, because we want to make a positive difference in other people's lives; ultimately, that's why we're here on this rock we call earth, isn't it? However, it also has the benefit of strengthening our own emotional health. Look for volunteer opportunities that focus on being with or directly helping other people.

Bear in mind that not every volunteer position is a social one. Working alone in a back room, doing things like stuffing envelopes, clerical work or manual labor, may be helpful to a non-profit organization (NPO), but it's not going to help you socially. With respect to this toolbox of social isolation, those types of things aren't going to have much of an impact. Instead, seek a more social volunteer placement with a well-known NPO in your community that has a long history and good reputation.

If you are just starting out in your career, volunteer work looks great on a resume. If you are unemployed, having a volunteer placement filling a gap on a resume looks far better than a gap in time that might be interpreted as laziness. In both cases, volunteer placements enhance your network of contacts and can sometimes lead to job offers. If you are retired and looking for a good way to spend some of your free time, volunteering is an excellent option. Depending on your background, your interests and your skills, you could find yourself doing anything from kitchen help at a local homeless mission to becoming a committee or board member for an NPO.

*If you are considering taking on volunteer work, be careful! **Run, don't walk, away** from any ad in social media, post on a community bulletin board or other request for volunteers, in cases where the organization has no history, cannot be verified, has no physical address, has a physical address in a dangerous area, is done from a private residence or has a shady reputation! Make sure that the place where you are volunteering is well-known in your community, that you will be working during daylight hours with other volunteers or staff, is at a location that is recognized as belonging to the organization and is legitimate. Avoid any volunteer situation that appears as though a for-profit business is merely getting free labor. Avoid going door-to-door and/or selling anything.

Introducing yourself in new social situations is the final tool in this toolbox. This might seem a bit like preaching to the choir, because people who are open to joining new groups, clubs and teams already do this, but something like the pandemic can make us forget to use our regular resources. If you're athletic, this is a no-brainer. Rejoin that beach volleyball, curling, golf, softball, sailing, rowing, skating, bowling… or whatever other type of team you enjoy as soon as your sport opens up once again.

Alternatively, there are endless other options for organized, regular social contact, including church groups (anything from bible study to choir), a position in your child's school council or participating in other ways. Consider an art-based club, book club, coaching, branded fitness community, pet-based groups, performance art community, campus clubs and much more. It's one thing to spend time doing a hobby or recreational activity on your own, but pursuing it in a group or club carries advantages of conversation, sharing your own ideas and getting new ideas from others. For example, an artist might enjoy the solitude, intense creative expression, peacefulness and maybe even emotional healing that occurs while painting watercolor art on her or his own; there's certainly a place for that. However, getting out and creating art in a group setting is an entirely different type of experience that can feed the soul in other distinctive ways. The laughter, conversation, smiles, creative ideas and encouragement, not to mention objective feedback, can result in great improvement in one's self-esteem, social capacity, creativity and positive demeanor.

Among all of the negative impacts that the Covid pandemic has wrought, social isolation is probably the easiest one to fix. You just need to put yourself out there in one form or another.

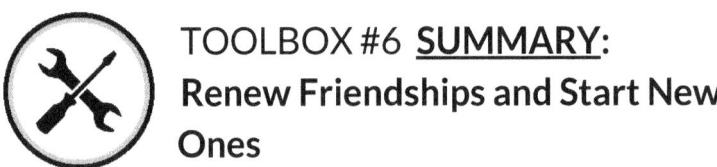

TOOLBOX #6 <u>SUMMARY</u>: Renew Friendships and Start New Ones

1. Reach out to others, even if they haven't made the effort.
Are you feeling timid about getting back together with friends and family in large gatherings or even intimate indoor settings? Many people continue to be stuck at this point, even though it's becoming increasingly safe to socialize again (obviously depending on where you live). Keep in mind that even though you may have moved on and are ready to being socializing again, it's possible that the people with whom you previously socialized are just not there yet. Whether that's the case or some of your social relationships have fallen between the cracks during the pandemic, don't wait for the invitation. Be the one who initiates the invitation. If you previously got together on an occasional or regular basis with a work or other social group for recreation, conversation or drinks, you might be the one who needs to get the ball rolling again!

2. It's a perfect time to edit your list of friends.
As we move through life's various stages of attending school or college, navigating our careers, being introduced to peers' friends and participating in various recreation, most of us gather

a group of social friends that may be rather eclectic. As the years pass, we may find that we have less and less in common with some friends. We realize this when spending time with them is increasingly uninteresting and brings little pleasure.

Other people on our long-standing social list may even prove to be unhealthy or toxic to our emotional well-being, sense of self-worth and sometimes even our physical safety. Sometimes we are partly to blame for relationships that leave us feeling worse than not having them at all. Stop trying to gain the attention, approval or acceptance of those who repeatedly push you away or who treat you as if you don't exist. They aren't worth your time or effort.

If the above descriptions fit anyone in your social pool, now would be a good time to do some editing. Any time is a difficult time to disassociate or drop individuals from our social list, even though it's the best thing to do. However, the pause on socializing that was created by the pandemic presents the perfect opportunity to take that step and trim those people from your list who no longer meet your emotional needs, bring little satisfaction or joy, or who negatively impact your emotional well-being. Focus, instead, on nurturing existing positive relationships and building new ones with people who are genuinely supportive and who respect you for who you are.

3. Call instead of text.

It's a proven fact that texting erodes our verbal communication skills and our ease with socializing. It's *so* much easier to simply tap in a few words and whoosh them to whomever, but it's also *so* much less effective at conveying the full meaning of your message. If you can't be there in person for real face-to-face communication, pick up the phone and call or use a real-time video phone app to carry-on a real-time visual conversation that is so much richer than mere words on a screen!

4. Get out of that cocoon and begin entertaining (again).

It's fairly easy to determine whether or not your neighbors would be considered keenly "social" people based on the number of non-family visitors they have over. Some people entertain others constantly, while others rarely, if ever, have anyone over. While some folks thrive on hosting a party or gathering, others are simply loners, don't want to make the effort or are really uncomfortable with everything that goes into putting on a get-together.

If Covid has flattened your 'dance card', so to speak, it's time to begin hosting small get-togethers once again. Start slow; keep it simple and casual! It might be more effort and stress than you remember. If you have always avoided having friends to your castle, they may feel resentful or wonder why you haven't, which doesn't exactly nurture relationships. Consider strengthening your social friendships by having a friend or couple over for a visit and see how it makes you feel; go from there. Suggestions for easy entertaining include simple meals like burgers and salads or a pot luck group effort, catering so you don't have to prepare any food, and casual attire so everyone feels at ease and comfortable.

5. Prepare conversation points in advance.

This tool may seem a bit over the top, but it can be extremely helpful in getting the ball rolling if or when conversation wanes and the ensuing silence becomes painfully awkward. This is especially applicable following almost two years of varying degrees of social isolation; in short, our social and conversational skills have become rusty!

Think, in advance, of conversation starters, topics in the news and funny stories that you can use. In mixed company, avoid the dreaded topics of religion and politics; dodge these subjects more than ever in today's divisive climate! People like talking about themselves, so gather some questions beforehand that you can ask about their lives, changes in what they're doing, their opinion on various things, etc. Listen attentively and ask more questions based on what they have to say.

Make a list of your conversation topics, starters and questions on your phone in case you forget them. You can always excuse yourself to the restroom to peek at your crib notes. You will likely be surprised by how well this works; so much so, that you'll want to make this a permanent part of preparing for social gatherings.

6. Help others who need it; become a volunteer.

In the first place, we volunteer to be altruistic; it's why we're here – to make a positive difference in other peoples' lives. However, there's a great fringe benefit; while you're helping others, you're helping yourself as well! If you're looking for a new volunteer role for the purpose of helping to reverse your own or someone else's social isolation, look for something that you would be doing with other people and not manual work in a corner or by yourself. There are some cautions discussed in the longer text of this toolbox with regard to seeking out and choosing a safe, legitimate and honest volunteer position. It is important that you read that advice for your own safety.

7. Join a new club, sport or group recreation community.

Boundless opportunities exist in just about any city or town when it comes to joining clubs, teams and groups. Think about your personal interests and hobbies; is there something that you enjoy doing on your own that is also offered in a group setting? If you are part of a couple, find out which groups welcome couples. The pandemic may have separated you from others for a finite period of time, but there are more enjoyable times ahead. Get out of the cocoon and do something that you enjoy in a group setting.

Toolbox #7
Reintroduce Structure And Routine

During the initial period of the pandemic, the workforce was divided in three. Essential workers reported to work as usual, while others began working from home and yet others stopped working altogether. The frontline workers and healthcare providers were pressed more heavily than ever before, both physically and emotionally. Students began learning remotely, while their teachers and professors taught from home or from makeshift classroom studios. Regardless of how it impacted your regular daily schedule, irregularity in terms of structure and routine became the norm.

Although a majority of the workforce has returned to the usual workplace, others are still not back to the normal pre-Covid routine. More employees than ever before were given the opportunity to work from home permanently and most of them went for it.

Some former employees simply chose not to return to work at all, leaving their jobs for an unknown future. Many of those who have returned to the physical workplace or other regular facility have noticed that, somehow, the structure and routine that defined pre-pandemic life and/or work, have not entirely returned. Plexiglas barriers, direction arrows on the floor, altered workspaces, cumbersome policies and various time-consuming procedures that seem futile; these changes have persisted, making things strange and surreal. It's been quite a challenge to feel like work is normal.

The pandemic changed everything from what time we wake in the morning, to when (or for some, *if*) we take a shower. The mid-pandemic stories of employees sitting at their computers in shirts and ties above the navel – and nothing but underwear or shorts below it – were amusing but quite common. People have observed that many workplaces seem to have undergone an apparel conversion, in which every day of the week has now become a "Casual Friday." As offices re-opened people in the U.S. and Canada reported more casual attire in professional settings than ever before, according to a recent survey by Captivate.[xxii] In that study, people in white collar settings reported seeing significantly more jeans, t-shirts, "athleisure wear" and even pajamas in the office compared to before the pandemic.

Although what you wear to work may or may not impact your productivity or effectiveness on the job, it does indicate that something has changed in terms of structure and routine. This apparel thing is only one of several indicators.

It's not just the workplace; many people are complaining that even though many aspects of life have returned to normal, life still doesn't *feel* normal. Part of the reason for this is that some of the structure and routine that contributed to the feeling of normality have changed and, in some cases, they are completely gone. If you are presently in such a mindset, it would be worthwhile and even healing to introduce things into your life that will provide structure and routine. Keep in mind that structure and routine are very important components of feeling in control of your life. This is an important point to remember!

Some practical things that anyone can do include planning your week in advance on the preceding weekend or planning your day the night before. Making a to-do list works wonderfully for giving our lives further purpose and helping to define areas of challenge and, subsequently, achievement. Maintain your daily routines regardless of how Covid has tried to change them. Make your bed every morning, eat a balanced diet of healthy unprocessed foods, set priorities (big and small), and leave time to care for yourself. In terms of attire, have you ever noticed that on your days off, the way you dress tends to set the tone for how you act and feel? When you choose your daily attire, ask yourself, "Would I be happy with what I'm wearing today if I ran into an old friend that I haven't seen for some time?"

Tend to any visual chaos in your home, yard or office. Visual chaos is not conducive to mental structure. If you have a lot of time on your hands, create regular theme days. For instance, each day could be dedicated to a certain overall task or activity. Schedule a date night and be creative with what that date might entail; hopefully something that you and your "someone special" both find appealing, interesting and fun! Many personal and life coaches suggest that you don't check your emails as soon as you get up and, similarly, that you try to avoid the inconsequential and time-wasting habit of looking at your phone. In this respect, it might be useful to download and install a safe screen usage tracker app on your phone and let it monitor how much time and how often you're spending on screen, as well as the types of activities in which you engage while you're paying all of that attention to your phone.

You might be astonished to discover how much time you're quite literally wasting on social media and other similar platforms. A recent study showed that the average American spent 608 hours on social media per year.[xxiii] On a global basis, people spend a bit more, with an average of 2 hours, 24 minutes per day, or 864 hours per year. Do the math. That's about an entire month of 24/7 social media use! Yikes! You could do a lot more with your time (and your life) if you could get into a routine and stop wasting so much time on such a meaningless pastime.

If you are among the unlucky ones who lost their job due to Covid, life feels far from normal. This is particularly true if you haven't managed to fill that gap with alternative employment or something meaningful. Feelings of anger, shock, sadness, reduced self-esteem, depression, frustration, desperation, fear, shame and fatigue are just some of the common emotional impacts that are associated with job loss. During a time of unexpected unemployment, particularly when extended, people often experience comorbid (multiple) emotional conditions. The pandemic exacerbated these emotions and feelings.

However, some people who temporarily or permanently lost their jobs as a result of Covid had a delayed emotional response. For the first several months, they didn't experience the shock and other emotional impacts. There were two reasons for this delayed response. First, the U.S. and Canadian governments, as well as several other economically privileged nations, provided varying levels and durations of emergency paycheck replacement aid for workers whose jobs were lost or paused. That monetary safety net not only helped people get by, it also softened the psychological blow. Second, the pandemic's distraction also softened the impact because some of those workers took comfort in the fact that tens of millions of other people were in the same predicament. For these people, the emotional crash was inevitable, but just postponed.

The primary solution to reduce the terrible feelings associated with job loss should be obvious, but it's often obscured because of those feelings. It can't be stressed enough that return to employment is crucial. Any employment? Well, in a sense, yes and no. Realistically, it would be unreasonable to expect a senior manager, executive or professional to take an interim job flipping burgers for minimum wage. Any potential gains to counter feelings of desperation and boredom would likely be overwhelmed with negative feelings of frustration, poor self-worth and anger due to having to take a job that is so dreadfully beneath one's qualifications, status and competence. It's an easy piece of advice to give, saying, "Just get a job – any job," but that can be terribly impractical and damaging to one's self-worth, depending on how much distance there is between the former position and the new one.

The solution for unemployed professionals and other workers whose qualifications, past experience and earning capacity are in the top 20% of the workforce, is to intensify the job search effort using multiple resources, including things like Linkedin.com queries and contacts, headhunters, direct applications and, of course, utilizing one's professional network. During this period of job search, it is crucial that the individual restore structure and routine as much as possible.

Waking up as early and consistently as one did prior to the job loss is key. Maintaining personal care, hygiene and proper attire are equally important. These individuals need to make and keep appointments for the regular business and life transactions that need attention. They also need to continue fostering their network of contacts, going to lunch or having meetings with those who are in a position to potentially assist. Meeting with former business and professional associates who may not be in a position to directly assist with the job search can still be very worthwhile, as it creates further structure, and forces one to "get out there." Doing so also shows others in the professional community that one is fit and ready to get down to business. These practices not only help to secure suitable employment; they also provide multiple benefits for emotional health.

If you remain unemployed or laid off because of the pandemic, but you do not have far to fall between your former employment and your current options, follow this advice. In these cases, take the lesser job *for now*. There are multiple advantages to doing this, including filling an otherwise awkward gap on a resume, demonstrating the work ethic to persevere in the face of challenges, making new contacts, discovering potentially new career options and, of course, helping to suppress or shed the negative emotional baggage associated with not being gainfully employed when one should be. Of course, during that stop-gap alternative employment, the worker should take advantage of opportunities to seek more suitable employment using an aggressive approach.

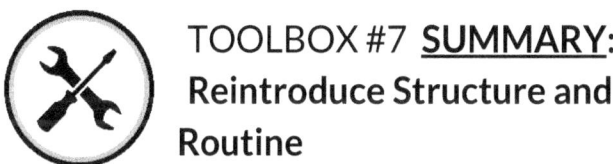

TOOLBOX #7 **SUMMARY**: Reintroduce Structure and Routine

1. Create or reintroduce a daily routine to your life that looks more like your pre-pandemic schedule.

2. Wake up early and consistently, and maintain personal care.
Make your bed and get yourself ready for the day before the day takes over. Attend to your personal hygiene, choice of apparel and breakfast as you normally would.

3. Make lists in advance.
Make daily lists the night before and weekly lists on the preceding weekend. Set priorities and include to-do's that

become challenges and, subsequently, achievements. *Planning and following through on your plans do wonders to reinstitute feelings of normality!*

4. Clean-up the visual chaos.
Put physical things away and where they belong. Visual chaos does not allow for a feeling of structure. Organize and feel good about your home, yard and office.

5. Set a regular date night.
Make regular date nights with your partner or someone close to you, planning to combine dinner or lunch with, perhaps other creative and interesting things that you both enjoy and find fun.

6. Prepare healthy meals and limit processed foods.
Eating junk food and overly processed, salty and fatty foods will make you feel sluggish and out of routine. Plan meals in advance; wondering what you're going to have for dinner a half hour before you're ready to eat leads to unhealthy options and negates feelings of normality.

7. Set theme days if you have a lot of time on your hands.
Select different days for specific types of activities or tasks. Stick to your days unless you find a better plan that fits with your schedule.

8. Limit your screen time.
Avoid checking emails as soon as you get up. Install a usage tracker on your phone to learn how much time you spend on certain screen activities and how often you access them. The average American spends close to a month of every year on social media, measured in 24/7 hours. This does not contribute to positive structure, routine or productive use of one's most precious resource; time.

9. If you are unemployed, ramp up the job search and/or take a job.
For those who were in the top echelon of the workforce in terms of professional skills, competencies and wage-earning capacity, taking a minimum wage low level job may not be the best remedy and may, in fact, introduce other emotional challenges. Ramp-up the professional job search using all relevant resources. Specific recommendations are provided in the earlier text in this toolbox. If the earning and skills gap between what you previously did for a living and a stop-gap job are not enormous, then it could be a good idea to take that job as a temporary measure while you actively search for something more suitable; the emotional and other benefits are significant.

10. Stay busy.
There are many biblical verses that warn against sloth and idleness, and whether or not you wish to follow their advice, there is ultimately much truth to the general idea that laziness, sluggishness and inertia are seriously not very good for humans!

Stephen J. Kristof

Toolbox #8
Get Out and Get Moving

There have been several references so far in this book about the importance of exercise and physical movement, and the positive impact that they can have on our general emotional state. When it comes to the feeling that the world around us seems unusual or strange and we can't seem to shake that feeling, the degree to which physical movement can help alleviate that sensation is simply remarkable! Mindfulness is a thinking technique wherein someone is aware of the present, the now, the moment. To be mindful, one needs to be aware of one's self and one's surroundings, including the environment and one's senses. Things seem far more normal and real when we are present in the moment. Grounding exercises are often recommended as easy methods to increase mindfulness. Doing things like splashing water on our face, focusing on our breathing, stretching and relaxing different parts of our body can all contribute to mindfulness.

However, in a more forceful sense, we also feel grounded when we engage in physical activity and exercise. Think about it; if you are working out vigorously on an elliptical, lifting weights, or running on the treadmill or on an outdoor path, you become quite conscious of your body and the reality of how it is interacting with the environment around you. Playing intense sports, of course, makes us extremely aware of our bodies in the moment and our thinking becomes quite grounded in what we are doing. If it's a competitive sport, we're totally focused on what we're doing to win. But getting out and moving doesn't have to be as intense as that. Playing a round of golf, going for a neighborhood stroll on a warm evening, discovering nature as you hike in a nearby park or forest; all of these mild-to-moderate physical activities can also do wonders for your body and your brain.

The key is to do *something* physical. Seasonal yard work is a good idea, because it usually involves a lot of bending, lifting, pulling, twisting and pushing. It also carries the distinct advantage of being outside, which is very important when you consider how much we were restricted to our indoor environment during the various pandemic lockdowns. Getting physical is awesome. Getting physical outdoors is even better!

During the winter between 2020 and 2021, an inventive practice grew in popularity with people using treadmills at home. People did virtual walks and runs "outside" by watching screens that mimicked the look and feel of walking or running in a variety of interesting and sometimes exotic outdoor locations. If you can, get outside for your physical exercise; if you cannot, congratulate yourself on staying active!

However, the added benefit of getting out is that it can help soothe the mind while we move our bodies in a new visual space, along with different sensations on our skin, new smells in the air and sounds of nature. Walking on a beach, along a hiking trail or in a nature sanctuary are truly beautiful experiences that can make life feel very 'real' and enjoyable. Cycling on new routes in rural areas can also be particularly freeing.

Another aspect of being outside while we exercise is less about the physical fitness angle and more about breaking free from the limited surroundings of our homes; something with which we became all too familiar during the pandemic. Even though you may not yet feel entirely comfortable with boarding a jet, train or bus, there are still plenty of ways you can get away and take in a different view. Consider taking a day trip to a neighboring city, county or rural area. When there, explore things that you normally wouldn't do. For example, if your nearby destination is already somewhat familiar, don't merely go there and expect it to do much for your mood! Ask yourself what a tourist would do if they visited the same place? Visit a museum or tourist-oriented venue and/or plan your stopover to coincide with a local seasonal festival or special event. Have a competition with your travel partner to see who can find the most new or interesting things about a not-too-far-away place that you thought you knew everything about!

If you can swing it, get away for a few days or longer. If traveling was an important part of your pre-Covid lifestyle, get back into that groove as travel becomes safer and more convenient. In short, getting out and moving will do wonders for your body, your mind and your disposition.

TOOLBOX #8 <u>SUMMARY</u>: Get Out and Get Moving

1. Make physical exercise or activity a priority.
Being grounded in the present does wonders for one's state of mind and helps to cultivate a much-needed sense of normalcy. One of the easiest ways to become grounded is to exercise our body. Engage in physical fitness that reflects your level of training, endurance and strength, as well as being suitable for your personal level of health.

Make and keep a commitment to physical movement every day. Avoid buying into the idea that exercise has to be intense in order to be beneficial! Just taking a 15-minute stroll every day of the week will do far more for one's health than not doing anything at all.

2. Move your fitness to an outdoor location.
Magnify the positive impact on your emotional state by moving outside. Doing yard work, hiking in a nature preserve, walking on trails, gardens and beaches, and cycling in rural locations can all contribute to normalcy and peacefulness. Just the fact that you are outside enhances mindfulness because of the multiple senses that are stimulated.

3. Take a day trip.
It doesn't have to be exotic or far away; just different. Get beyond the four walls that you've become all too familiar with and change your scenery. Plan to visit a neighboring city or town and approach it as a new tourist would. Create a challenge game with your travel partner to find as many new things as possible; the prize for the winner is as limitless as your imagination!

4. Experienced travelers should feed that hunger as soon as safely possible.
If you've put off that trip to Europe or somewhere exotic, stop talking about it and set a plan in motion. You don't have to travel today or even next year, but look toward a future without Covid and commit to making it happen. If there's a destination that's become a tradition in your family, maybe a family cottage, vacation rental or lodge that gives you the warm and fuzzies, go as soon as you are able to or make plans so that you have something else to look forward to.

Stephen J. Kristof

Toolbox #9
Keep Up Appearances

    Imagine that you're on your way to a social gathering hosted by a couple of your close friends. Let's call them Terry and Trevor. It's been a while since you've attended any party, so although you're really looking forward to it, you're also a bit apprehensive. Three other couples are expected to attend who you also know well, so there will be plenty of people to strike-up conversation with; you anticipate many laughs and interesting stories as the evening progresses. Oh, and then there's the food! Trevor is the king of barbecue and Terry is the quintessential pastry chef. They have always thrown the best parties and are the perfect hosts. Even though you're a bit envious, you love going there because their home and yard always look stunningly gorgeous.

    It's been a long, difficult pandemic and now that everyone is safe and we can move on with life, this is the first thing you've looked forward to in a long time. As you pull up to their driveway, you notice that something is different. You can't quite put your finger on it, but their house just doesn't seem to have the same sparkle that it used to have. You notice that the landscaping is rough and shrubs haven't been trimmed in some time. Kids toys are strewn about the yard and the lawn appears to have been hastily mowed just hours ago; you realize that the grass must have been very long, because there are ugly clumps of it everywhere, including on the driveway. Another couple's SUV is already in the driveway, which makes you a bit less nervous and happy that you're not the first person there!

    Ding Dong. As you ring the bell, Terry opens the door and you are, well…shocked. Her straggly hair has gone grey from the top of her head to the middle, she's wearing a raggedy old sweatshirt and wrinkly jeans, and it looks like she forgot to put on any makeup. "Oh well," you think, "I'm not going to be so shallow as to judge her appearance; it's what's inside that counts."

It's a nice thought, but as you look around their normally spotless house, you feel a bit embarrassed for the couple. They appear to have forgotten how to put things away and how to clean. Everything is literally everywhere and you're seriously starting to have second thoughts about coming. As you walk through the kitchen to get a drink, you notice that the countertop is glazed with what appears to be raw meat drippings, orange juice and who knows what else. You get sick to your stomach when you see some cheese crumbs and realize that the assortment of cheeses that you were just nibbling from the charcuterie board was sliced on this same counter. At this point you're already worried about ingesting any other appetizer, let alone the main course!

Trevor enters from the patio doors wearing a funny paper chef's hat and a grilling apron embroidered with the phrase, "Born to Grill." He smiles broadly and embraces you with a big old bear hug. He's genuinely happy to see you, but you were not prepared for the odor; apparently Trevor has forgotten what soap and shampoo look like.

Okay, the story is a bit lengthy and super obvious, but it does paint a disappointing picture, doesn't it? The point is that, even though we've lived through a nearly two-year pandemic, along with all of the restrictions and emotional baggage that it brought, life does go on and we move along with it. However, that doesn't mean that we should lower our standards of appearance and preparation just because we've lived through a pandemic. Some of the dynamics of the pandemic, such as the social isolation, working from home, not working at all, lack of motivation and/or hopelessness led many of us to accept a decline in our personal standards of appearance for both ourselves and our surroundings. Many people still complain that they just don't have it in them to clean the house or yard any more. Similar feelings migrated to a lack of incentive to keep up our own personal appearances. Some people joked that the same pair of sweatpants and 1970's rock band t-shirt became their daily pandemic "uniform"!

As humorous as that sounds, it was and continues to be a reality for many people. Now, before you go and judge the anecdote at the beginning of this toolbox as sounding shallow and, perhaps, even misogynistic, elitist or outdated, this isn't intended to promote dyed hair over grey hair, cosmetics over a natural look, formal apparel over more casual clothing, or a pretentiously dazzling home over one that is clean, but comfortably lived in.

The real message here is that, IF we cared about the appearance of ourselves and our surroundings prior to the pandemic <u>and we have since lost the impulse to care</u>, it is a potential red flag for depression and social withdrawal. It also doesn't help us feel "normal" the way that we did when we cared about these things. Sure, there's a freedom in not caring about what other people think about our personal appearance, but if the real reason for letting our appearance, hygiene and cleanliness slip is because we no longer have the drive or willingness to do so, it could paint a bigger picture of malaise, depression and social withdrawal.

If, on the other hand, the pandemic has caused you to focus on the things that are truly important in life and you now realize that some of your former habits were pretentious, that's an entirely different story. For some people, that's a big step forward and they should be applauded for coming to that realization and for choosing to tame their fixation on outward appearance. That does not mean, however, that we should also disregard hygiene, cleanliness and an overall appearance that denotes self-respect. This also applies to our living spaces. Don't throw out the baby with the bathwater.

This discussion gets a bit sticky at this point, because people who have healthy self-esteem are accepting of who they are and how they look. They like what they see when they look in the mirror and are less apt to criticize. If they see something that they would like to tweak, they make a positive decision to change what they can, such as hair style or color, targeted exercise or eating more healthfully, but they see these things as pliable; ultimately, they are happy with how they look. When it comes to visible difference or other physical appearances that may not be reflected in our image-oriented society, they have a healthy body image; they're comfortable and pleased with how they look.

However, since body image is tied to self-esteem, we also recognize that someone who has high self-esteem and a healthy body image, is more likely to dress in such a way as to promote their happiness with how they look. People with these positive traits tend to avoid going out in public looking like a slob. They realize that the way that they care for themselves and what they wear is, in part, a reflection of their self-esteem.

Commonly, when an individual experiences depression and poor self-esteem, it's reflected in their physical appearance. They sometimes avoid proper personal hygiene, and wear clothing and hairstyles that appear ill-fitting, unkempt or dull. This is why it's important that you don't confuse maintaining a good outward appearance with being overly focused on society's obsession with airbrushed perfection. That's not at all what is suggested.

If you want to feel like life is normal again, you need to reflect normalcy in all aspects of how you live your life, not just in selected ones. It's also not the time to stop doing certain things just because you now realize that they take too much time or energy. The tools in this second last toolbox are the simplest of all, yet they are very important in getting your emotional groove back.

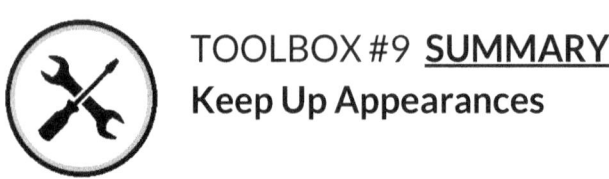

TOOLBOX #9 SUMMARY: Keep Up Appearances

1. Tend to your personal appearance and hygiene.
Shortly after waking, start your day in the right direction by showering, tending to your hygiene and hair, and choosing apparel that says, "I am going to look great today!" You are not doing it for others, as much as you are doing it for yourself. Healthy levels of self-respect and emotional balance are tied to our personal appearance.

2. Always remind yourself, "You never know who I'm going to run into!"
Dressing, shaving, cosmetics – whatever you need to do to look good – do it as though you may unexpectedly meet a long-lost friend, prospective new employer, potential new romantic partner or former classmate. This doesn't mean that you need to pander to society's obsession with perfection! It simply means that you've given thought and care to your appearance. When meeting that unexpected person, most people would want to project an image that says, "I am happy, well-adjusted, self-assured and confident."

3. Clean your home, clean your yard.
Whether you live in a sprawling estate, a simple bungalow, a condo, apartment or townhouse doesn't matter. Keep your surroundings clean and tidy. Put things where they belong. If you can't get things organized because the clutter is overwhelming, pull the plug and start dumping with abandon!

There's a thought out there that we should pitch whatever we have not used in five years and whatever else does not make us happy. Visual clutter leads to cluttered minds and emotions. Straighten it out.

4. Update your home décor.
This and the next tool require money. If you are financially able to do so, consider updating some of the décor in your home that now looks passé, kitsch or dull. If you were considering a home renovation prior to the pandemic, put it in motion. You may find that contractors are extremely busy, with some booking up to and beyond a year in advance, so it's a good idea to get on it. Even if you have to wait a while, at least you will have some concrete plans and something to look forward to.

5. Update your wardrobe.
Again, it's a cash dependent option, but if you can swing it, now is a good time to give your outdated apparel a new look. This is particularly important if you are just starting out or are in the thick of your career and are looking to advance. Look the part if you want to play the part! Beyond the career perspective, modernizing our wardrobe tends to give us an emotional lift.

Toolbox #10
Repair Your Relationships

As noted in Chapter 4, many relationships have been pushed to the breaking point due to the tremendous stresses of the pandemic. In many households, spousal, parent-child and sibling relationships have deteriorated significantly since the start of the pandemic. Part of the blame goes to the added tension that Covid created in terms of worries about health, unemployment, financial distress and daily life in general. Also to blame is the amount of time that people have been spending together due to lock-downs, restrictions, working and learning from home, and having far fewer recreation and entertainment options.

It's no secret that many families have experienced a great deal of friction throughout the pandemic. Although occasional clashes between spouses and between parents and children are quite normal in any family, Covid drove some deep wedges into many families, with the clashes being more frequent and out of character than what would normally be expected. As a result, many relationships that were struggling prior to the pandemic are now further damaged and broken, while other relationships that were previously holding their own are now weaker than they were. They may be in disrepair, but that doesn't necessarily mean that these relationships are beyond repair. At the very least, they can be strengthened.

The negativity that results from disagreement and fighting within a family can permeate one's daily thoughts, interfering with everything from health to career. Most certainly, it can also take a heavy toll on relationships. It's time to take stock of our relationships once the pandemic is in the rear-view mirror. If damage was done and you feel like you need to lay blame, then blame the pandemic. Do not, however, blame the other person in the relationship.

It's important for us to realize our own responsibility in a deteriorated relationship, regardless of whether or not we feel we are to blame. You are not super-human and, like everyone else, it's extremely unlikely that your mood, your behavior and your interactions with those around you were not impacted by Covid. They were. You, along with all of us, experienced feelings of shock, anxiety, frustration, anger and maybe even depression due to events of the past few years.

The question to ask yourself is **not whether** you were abrupt, impatient, angry or frustrated with your spouse, children, sibling or parent; instead, ask yourself **to what extent** you were like this. Yes, they may have behaved like this to you as well, but now is not the time to cast blame. Explore what *you* can do to repair or strengthen your damaged relationships and put some measures in play. No matter what you do, keep it positive and look forward. Assume that *you* need to change; identify how you have contributed to the weakened relationship(s) and fix what needs to be addressed. Don't expect your strategies to make everything whole in short order; the deeper the hurt, the longer it will take.

Now is the time to let it all go; put it in the past along with all of the other negative baggage. We'd all like to tell Covid to pack its bags and get lost. Make sure that all of the blame and negativity that ended-up hurting relationships also gets packed into those bags and gets lost forever. Let it go and move toward a brighter future with stronger, happier, more fulfilling relationships.

Another relationship that many people have not even considered through this pandemic is our relationship with God. If you are not the religious or spiritual type, this advice is obviously not going to be on your personal agenda. No harm, no foul intended; there are dozens of other helpful strategies as you move through this book. However, if you do consider yourself to have a personal relationship with God *(what more personal relationship could there be?)*, then perhaps you could examine that relationship from the perspective of how it has fared through the pandemic? Without doubt, some people's faith has intensified during this period, due to a number of circumstances. Many others, though, may be feeling that the connection has lately been a bit shaky.

For those who attended religious services on a regular basis prior to the pandemic, but were forced to stop attending, the resulting void may be impacting their faith or feeling of connectedness. As safety returns, starting to attend services again will help fill that void, can provide comfort and can reconnect. In another way, some people have been so focused on calamity and have felt so unsettled for such an extended period of time that it has impacted their spiritual sense of hope.

Reinstating prayer, practicing meditation and focusing on thankfulness are excellent ways to restore faith and hope. Here are some specific things you can do to reach that place.

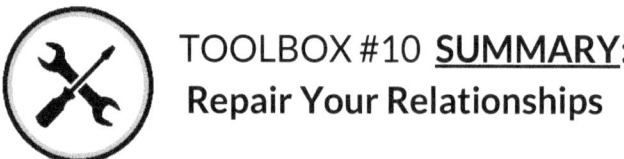

TOOLBOX #10 **SUMMARY**: Repair Your Relationships

1. Let it go.
Refuse to participate in the blame game. That does nothing but perpetuate greater hurt, anger and division. If your partner in the relationship is stuck at the blame stage, it's probably best to accept, don't argue and move on. If It's so important for him or her to feel like they are in the right and have to 'win' every argument, it's highly unlikely they will accept anything other than victory when it comes to who's at fault for the rocky road. Instead of wasting your time, put your energy into positive things that move the relationship in a new and better direction.

2. Recognize and come to terms with the pandemic's impact on your relationship.
A good starting point is to have a frank discussion about the ways in which the pandemic has affected you and your counterpart. Start a conversation, using parts of this book to help reflect on the various ways that Covid has put tremendous

strain on *everyone's* emotional health. Try to come to an understanding that your 'team' has been under a lot of pressure and focus on the positive, in that you both don't want Covid to win any more by taking hold of your relationship and destroying it.

3. Plan diversion and recreation activities that you both enjoy.

If you're like most of us, you've put off many enjoyable plans and activities that previously made life fun and that helped bring a spark to your relationship. As restrictions loosen and safety increases, plan and engage in activities that you both look forward to doing together. Re-book that special vacation; if you must, scale it down or keep it more local if you're just not ready to travel yet. Start a new paired hobby, or join a club or team that allows couples to participate. Go on day some day trips. Play a board game together if you haven't done so in a while. Plan to go out with social friends or have them over, as long as that doesn't add any more tension to your life or to your relationship.

It's really important to spend quality, face-to-face time with each other, but since we've all been stuck at home for so long, it's important for that face-to-face time to be somewhere else if at all possible.

4. Find a suitable relationship therapist.

This isn't exclusively for couples; relationship therapists work with all sorts of arrangements, including parent-child, sibling-sibling, etc. If you feel that the depth of your relationship trouble is beyond your own capacity to fix it, getting help from a qualified professional could make the difference. Of course, the only way this ever works is for both parties to not only agree, but to *embrace* it as a genuine *opportunity*.

Encourage an atmosphere where you both want to look toward a happier future; this way the process may seem more palatable than if it's presented as a last resort to fix our problems.

You may also consider talking with your pastor, priest, rabbi, cleric or other religious leader for advice and counsel. In many cases, one marital partner may be far more amenable to seeing a religious counselor who they already know and trust, rather than a complete stranger who they know nothing about. Of course, if a traditionally taboo subject is part of the problem, some partners may be too embarrassed and would rather speak with a layperson. However, keep in mind that most religious leaders have heard it all; however awful you think the problem is, it's not new to them at all.

5. Become a good communicator.
Some of the worst wars in history were caused by unintentional blunders in communication. Some of the best relationships in the world were fostered on effective communication. Start focusing on effective communication techniques in your relationship. Don't merely talk about listening; actively do it. Put away the phone and turn-off the TV. Listen attentively to your relationship partner, whether it be your spouse or child; this is both respectful and tremendously constructive. Expect the same respect from them.

Ask more questions than you answer. Ask questions based on what they have just said; this not only keeps the conversation ball rolling fluidly, but also reassures your partner that you are actually listening to and taking interest in what they are saying.

LOOK AT EACH OTHER while you talk with each other. Look into his or her eyes; this, in itself, can be a very effective way of enhancing a relationship! Ask what they are planning to do for the day and ask if there's anything that you can do to help or to make them happy. Ask how their day went.

6. You fell in love some time ago; now it's time to stay in love.

Falling in love is an entirely different thing from keeping the love going. The second one is, admittedly, much harder; it takes time, effort, creativity, patience and sacrifice. When you think about it, falling in love with someone requires none of those things! Some things you can do to keep the love light burning brightly are to find out and re-learn what your partner likes and dislikes; similarly, you should also express the same things and don't make them guess.

Work on the sacrifice part. We all become selfish in our relationships over time. We take our partner for granted and tend to blame them for things that did not work out as planned. We often ignore what they do for us and focus, instead, on what they neglect to do. Yet, when faced with decisions that require more give than take, we're often less eager to give as much as we take. Do something with or for your partner that means a great deal to them or that just makes them happy, even if it doesn't rate highly on your list of things you want to do.

Just like a plant needs fertilizer to thrive, feed your relationship. It will not flourish or even survive without the essentials. If you ignore the plant, it will wither; if you ignore your relationship, it will too. Be creative in showing him or her that you love them! Whether you say it 100 times a day or just once, merely saying, "I love you," is meaningless if you don't show and live it on a daily basis. Ask yourself how you can show your love in a new and inventive way and choose a day to do it.

7. If you don't feel "in love" anymore, try loving more.
Finally, one of the most common reprises heard during couples therapy is the phrase, "I don't love him/her anymore." Whether the pandemic made you feel this way or it occurred, bit by bit, over a longer term, one of the most effective remedies for this problem is to *love your partner*.

If you don't feel in love your partner, ask yourself, honestly, how much are you *trying* to love them? Show compassion when they need it. Don't merely congratulate them; rather, try to feel joy for their accomplishments and achievements. At the same time, avoid being merely sympathetic when they fall or fail; instead, be empathetic and feel their sadness. Compliment your partner regularly and specifically.

Look for the qualities and other things about your partner that you fell in love with in the first place. The things you initially admired about your partner are likely still there; perhaps they're somewhat obscured by the time that's passed and everything that has occurred during those years, but it's likely worth the effort to look for them.

8. Restore your spiritual relationship.
If you consider yourself to be a spiritual person, here's a very important question to ask yourself regarding the pandemic and spirituality. Did the pandemic strengthen or weaken your spirituality and your connectedness to God?

As a spiritual person, one easily recognizes how crucial our relationship with God is to our personal feeling of normality. Not only that, this connection brings tremendous reassurance in the face of worry and uncertainty. People with strong spirituality are also more apt to experience and share feelings of peace, joy and love.

If you feel that the pandemic has weakened your connection to God, make it a priority in your life to restore that connection through more committed and regular practice of prayer and meditation and devotion.

Stephen J. Kristof

Chapter 6

Healing From Loss

We all experienced loss in one form or another during and due to Covid-19. When we first heard the term "Coronavirus" most of the globe's population had no idea what it would lead to and how much it would cost. Much of this was collateral damage, but we were also unprepared for the direct damage in the loss of loved ones and friends who succumbed to the virus. Regrettably, by the beginning of November, 2021, the world lost over 5,000,000 people to Covid, while the U.S. lost over 750,000. Although the global deaths figures are staggering, they may be even worse. Experts suggest that the overall numbers have been grossly underreported due to some world governments' resistance to reporting accurate data, as well as the fact that some other nations have had little to no testing or protocols for testing.

The domestic numbers are so large that it's likely Covid hit close to home for most people. Many people reading this book lost a close family relative or friend, or at least personally knew someone who suffered a similar loss. In fewer cases the loss was compounded as yet another family member died from Covid. Such tragic stories like this are hard to come to terms with. Grieving the death of someone you were close to is never an easy process, but some experts have found that if Covid was responsible for the passing, it augmented the difficulty for some of the bereaved. This is in part due to the stark isolation that was common to the way in which patients died. In most cases, loved ones and friends were not permitted to be physically with the dying patient, which also meant that the patient had to die alone or with a non-family medical attendant.

There was also a lack of some of the customary elements that lead to a sense of closure. During some of the pandemic waves, funeral homes and places of worship were prohibited from hosting viewings or services at all or beyond a very small number of immediate family members. Some funeral homes switched to virtual online proceedings, but they were often strange and upsetting. Many bereaved families chose to put off their loved ones' funerals, choosing instead to cremate remains of the deceased, to be held at home or at the funeral home until a future date when a more proper funeral, internment or memorial could be held. Certain religions and denominations do not permit such a delay, so those families did not have a choice.

The fact is that losing someone due to any cause of death during the pandemic brought far more stress, sadness and confusion to the bereaved than they would have already experienced during normal times. It also interfered with a sense of closure. For those who lost a loved one to the ravages of Covid-19, those terrible feelings were multiplied exponentially.

Grief is a difficult and complex process to work through. Many people have heard about the five stages of grief; some newer theories suggest that grieving process has between 7 and 12 components. In 1969, Dr. Elisabeth Kübler-Ross, a Swiss psychiatrist, identified the five stages of grief as being: Denial, Anger, Bargaining, Depression and Acceptance. The problem with these condensed stages, as well as with the extended 12 stage model is that they are often presented to bereaved individuals as a path that they should expect to experience fully and in a linear fashion. In reality, a person rarely experiences these stages or waves along a linear path. Even Kübler-Ross corrected this misinterpretation of her theory, stating that the stages are not experienced on a straight, continuous path and that some people may experience only a few stages or possibly none of them at all. However, identifying a certain stage or emotion that a bereaved person is experiencing can be very useful in helping them to understand that what they are feeling is valid, expected and typical. The problem arises when the bereaved individual has actually worked through their grief, but still has the expectation that further waves of grief are imminent because they never experienced them.

Whether someone lost a loved one to Covid during the pandemic or to some other cause, the pandemic itself likely contributed to greater difficulty dealing with the grief. Mentally processing the death of a loved one and eventually getting on with life is hard enough, but consider that during the pandemic there were several factors that made it even more arduous. There were far fewer distractions; many people who previously worked outside the home were working at home or not working at all. They were socially isolated from their regular support systems. As well, the plethora of restrictions made life seem even more unreal than it normally does when someone close passes.

Understanding, then, that the traditional stages of grief are not experienced along a straight line and that not everyone experiences some or any of them, how can we make sense of what we're going through? It's important to note that there is no "right" way to grieve! Everyone experiences grief differently. Some people cry endlessly for months, while others hardly shed a tear. Many people are severely impacted in terms of their sleep, eating and waves of panic, while others transition quickly to a new life without the deceased and move on. For most people, it's easier to separate the grieving process into two major phases; the initial period is known as the <u>acute</u> stage, while the following period is known as the <u>integrated</u> stage.

During the initial period, most people experience a range of intense emotions and physical manifestations that *may* include feelings such as shock, sadness, guilt, loss of appetite, loss of libido, restlessness, sleeplessness, irritability, and waves of emotional and physical distress. In terms of how long this phase lasts, it varies for everyone. Don't forget that we all process difficult life situations differently; some of us are extremely resilient and tend to bounce back quickly from everything. Regardless, if you take longer to heal then that's what you need. The circumstances surrounding the death also impact the grieving process. The difference between losing someone following a long and painful journey, and that of a sudden, unexpected death are significant and set forth different types of feelings and emotional hurdles. For example, when a loved one finally comes to rest after enduring a long battle with a debilitating disease, the bereaved may initially feel a sense of relief and peace. However, sometimes that same person can later experience feelings of guilt about the earlier sense of relief. As you can see, the circumstances of death can create different emotional responses in the grieving process, so no one model applies universally.

The dynamics of the relationship shared between the bereaved and the deceased also have a considerable influence on feelings experienced during the grieving process and the length of that process. The grieving process becomes more complicated when there are unresolved issues in a relationship, unfulfilled promises or important sentiments that were never communicated.

Maybe there were no issues like these, but, instead, the relationship was beautiful and intense. When this is the case, we miss the deceased with such passion that it often initially feels as though we can't go on without them. Grieving is less about missing someone than it is about learning how to eventually go on living without their physical presence in our lives. The fact is that they will *always* be a big part of our lives moving forward. We will always miss someone who was important to us. The closer our relationship with that person, the more we will continue to miss them. But it eventually becomes less painful and, as we come to terms with their physical loss, our emotions become buoyed by beautiful memories. We can ultimately integrate that yearning into our lives as we move forward; moving on in increasingly positive and less painful ways.

The healing described in the last paragraph represents the second major phase of grieving; the integrated stage. During this time, the bereaved begins to learn how to carry on with life, integrating the loss into regular aspects of living life. Grief becomes less painful and healing ensues. The heartache never really goes away, but becomes far more manageable and the grief is no longer incapacitating. There's no telling how long it takes for anyone to move from the acute to the integrated stage. For many people it's measured in months.

However, when the pain of grieving continues intensely and with debilitating impact beyond months and starts to be measured in years, the individual may be experiencing a third phase of complicated grief, which was identified in 2014 as Prolonged Grief Disorder (PGD).[xxiv] If you have continued for a year or longer to experience painful grief and have found it difficult to cope and get on with life, you could be stuck in a state of complicated grief. Know that, as difficult as it is to believe, healing is not only possible, but will occur. However, individuals experiencing complicated grief need psychological or psychiatric support in order to initiate that healing. Restoration-focused treatments may include individual or group psychotherapy. The key is to have the awareness to recognize that the severe grief has gone on for too long and the courage to choose to do something about it. As noted, fortunately, help is available and you can take your life back. That doesn't mean that you are shutting-out your loved one who has passed. On the contrary, it means that you can begin living life again, while integrating the loss, the memories and the spirit of your loved one into your life in less painful ways.

Here are some strategies that may help someone transition from the acute to the integrated phase of grief:

Recognize and Accept the Reality of Your Loss. Grieving cannot be erased by merely willing it to go away. It does take time and can't be rushed. Thinking about what the loss means to you emotionally and intellectually is an important step. Understand that the pain you are feeling is real and can have both emotional and physical manifestations. You are not alone; everyone has to deal with grief during their lives. What you are feeling is very real. The intensity of these feelings will initially fluctuate without reason or warning, but that intensity will eventually subside.

Confront Your Emotions; Even the Painful Ones. There may be realities in terms of some really negative feelings that you simply have to face and process. Things like guilt, fear, sadness, anger, depression, heartbreak and disorganization are common and should not be ignored if you experience any them. You may not experience a particular emotion; grieving is a highly individual process. Should you have them, accept that these negative emotions are real; name them and learn to cope with them.

You are not a superhero. Give yourself the comfort and time that you know you need to get through this. Look after yourself emotionally and physically. Even though you may have lost your appetite, understand that your body needs proper nutrition and you cannot heal emotionally without a strong and healthy body. One impacts the other. Accept support from friends and loved ones who offer it. Try not to shut yourself out from other people. You do need time to yourself, but not all of the time.

Think about how your life has changed and will change. Do this when you are able to begin processing these thoughts. There will be adjustments in your life; it's inevitable. Often, when we are with someone for a long time, our identity and theirs become intertwined and it's hard to think about how we fit into a new identify without our partner. Practical responsibilities will also need some adjustment. Routines, work and caring for others may also be different. The way you see the world and your understanding of spiritual concepts may have also changed. Change in itself is a difficult concept for many people, but it is a necessary thing in order for most people to move on and, often, to move into a better place. Be willing to accept change as a means to live a life that's less painful, that makes more sense and that allows you to experience happiness.

Write about your thoughts, experiences and memories. Writing about the thoughts that you have will help you recognize things that need to be resolved and things that are part of who you are as you move through this process. It will also validate your negative feelings, which will help you move beyond them. Writing about the difficulties that you are experiencing will help you understand what is happening to you and may help you make connections. Writing about memories of your loved one will help you focus on those bittersweet moments and shared experiences that will eventually become less bitter and far sweeter.

Continue to talk about, think about and memorialize your loved one. Ignoring them will not reduce your pain and will not help you move through a necessary process. Instead, encourage others in your life to share positive memories of your loved one and to celebrate their life.

Give Your Grief to God. If prayer, spiritual observances and religious traditions or sacraments have fed your soul and sustained emotional balance through the years, it would be foolish to avoid leaning on them during a time of grief. Share your feelings, thoughts and struggles through prayer. Meditate on the good memories; express gratitude in your spiritual communication for the gift of your loved one and for how they impacted you positively while they were here. Ask God for help to ease the pain of grief.

Chapter 7
Resilience

How would you rate your emotional resilience? The answer could provide a window into how you respond to various crises in your life, from the tiny everyday stuff to the biggies. Your resilience may have a lot to do with your post-pandemic emotional state. Throughout this book, a variety of coping tools have been provided to help get your life back to normal. It's entirely possible that the value of these strategies will resonate with you to the degree that you adopt many of them to be a healthy part of your post-pandemic life. They may even enhance your resilience to more promptly rebound and move on.

Prior to the pandemic, what was your customary pattern in dealing with the small stuff? How did you usually react to minor challenges and struggles; the everyday obstacles and worries that are a part of everyone's lives? Did mundane uncertainties or simple complications frequently set your day aflame? If this sounds silly, be thankful that your constitution remains solid when negative things confront you. Generally speaking, people who have a high degree of resilience against the small struggles in life are also surprisingly adept at deflecting or effectively dealing with the more challenging situations. They also tend to bounce back rapidly and with ease.

However, we're not all like this. Recognizing that hardships and challenges create undue anxiety is a positive thing. Likewise, acknowledging that you have difficulty returning to normal also allows for change and growth. It's certainly not something that should cause you any shame or guilt. We all have deficiencies or weaknesses that make life more difficult, but the good thing is that some of those limitations can be improved, with the result being a less difficult and more enjoyable life.

Fortunately, resilience is one of those things that can be learned and improved. So, you're not Superman or Wonder Woman! You are also not perfect. Guess what? The people you look up to as role models of grace under pressure because of their tough as nails responses to rough times, well, they aren't likely as calm or resilient as they would like you to believe. Everyone has a public face; in many cases, it's a highly polished façade that protects weakness and vulnerability.

The public face that you see among Hollywood actors is just part of their story! While the tough guy and bravado-oriented images are hard to play down, countless very well-known actors admit that their off-screen personalities are far from their studio-packaged personas. Some of them who have played the world's most ruthless villains and others who portray sophisticated agents are rather shy, mild-mannered and somewhat anxious individuals in real life.

There's no question that we've been programmed to believe in the media's standard for physical beauty and strength of character. We live in a *Photoshop Culture*. The media feeds us a never-ending stream of so-called "perfection" in the form of celebrities, actors and influencers. Remove the Photoshop retouching, plastic surgery, perfect lighting, carefully crafted messages from professional publicists and strategically staged appearances, and what's left over is nothing like the "reality" that we were led to believe. Most of the people that you know, most people that everyone knows, don't even come close to that standard, and the reason is because most people don't actually look like that.

We've also been programmed to have a false expectation of perfect mental health and emotional stability in ourselves and in those around us. Many of us actually believe that average people don't occasionally fight feelings of anxiety, depression, confusion, lethargy, self-doubt and a host of other upsetting states of mind. However, this is simply not true. Average people – the people we live around, work with, do business with and socialize with - _do_ have episodes of emotional distress and they may experience them more frequently than you or I. As far as the celebrities, despite their carefully managed images and emotionally stable appearance, a far greater proportion of celebrities attend regular therapy than do average people. In fact, the extreme stress of keeping up their artificial appearance is often one of the reasons that so many famous people need to attend therapy.

The fact is that WE ALL experience these feelings from time to time. It also takes everyone a lot more time and effort to bounce back from difficult episodes than they want you to realize. Think about it; how often have you felt absolutely dreadful after a serious pitfall or loss, but when asked how you're doing by coworkers, friends or even relatives, your response is almost always far more cheerful than you actually feel? Now consider that if you do this, so does everyone else!

"Call it what you will, pride, ego or preserving our reputation; we want to appear more resilient than we actually are."

Although the media is partly to blame due to their promotion of celebrities as icons of beauty and mental health stability, our human nature also bears some responsibility in this regard. We generally put our guard up after suffering a loss, rather than allowing others to see how badly we've been hurt or damaged.

Call it what you will, pride, ego or preserving our reputation; we want to appear more resilient than we actually are.

Yet another factor has contributed to our desire to cover up our hurt. If you were a product of the Baby Boom generation or even the next Gen-X cohort, you were likely brought up with abundant doses of, *"Don't let them see you sweat," "Don't let them see you cry,"* and *"Keep a stiff upper lip"* types of messaging and expectations. You would have experienced even more intense messaging if you were a male growing up during that time period. Our culture has taught us that admitting to our hurt or difficulty is a sign of weakness. Do you remember the term, "Cry Baby?" If so, osmosis likely caused you to be caught up in a similar indoctrination.

In our society, imperfection is frowned upon and weakness is resisted. We are also focused on presenting an image that is stronger, more attractive and more successful than we actually are. As a result, when we are faced with a tragedy or pitfall that drags us down, we avoid admitting that we are in pain and don't ask for help, for fear that others may discover that we're just human. Worse, yet, is the fact that we're embarrassed; we feel shame and experience guilt because we're having trouble bouncing back to normal. This is extremely common, but most people are reluctant to admit it. Accepting that we are human and that we are not as resilient as we'd like to be is a good thing. There's no question that some people are more resilient than you, but there are a lot more people like you than you probably realize. Accept this weakness as something that is common and that is changeable. Be willing to accept the help, support and guidance of true friends, and to seek-out professional help if needed. Know that resilience is like a muscle that can be conditioned and strengthened! The good news is that whether it was the pandemic that has knocked you back a bunch of pegs, an unrelated event or a combination of things, you are stronger than you realize.

What are the signals that indicate that your resilience is low? The following experiences and characteristics may indicate that your resilience could use a tune-up:

- **Lack of Hope or Vision for the Future;** despair and feeling that there is nothing to look forward to or that things will not get better

- **Recurring or Persistent Physical Illness;** weak mental resilience can impact physical immunity, making us more vulnerable to colds and various ailments

- **Inflammation;** in a similar fashion, reduced immunity due to low resilience often leads to inflammation in muscles, joints and other parts of the body

- **Prone to Crying and Depressive State;** crumbling into tears for no reason or due to insignificant circumstances

- **Isolating Ourselves;** removing ourselves purposefully from regular social situations and/or groups because we don't want people to see how poorly we are doing

- **Difficulty Remembering Things;** confusion and brain fog that accompany low resilience make it hard to remember even simple things

- **Becoming Overly Clingy to One or More People;** feeling that a person or people are necessary for your continued functioning

- **Sleep Disturbance or Deprivation;** it is difficult to sleep for more than an hour or two without waking and when we do, it's even more difficult to get back to sleep; the sleep we do get is stressed and rough, sometimes resulting in the feeling that we need a good night's sleep right after waking

- **Overreacting to Trivial Stress;** everyday things can set us off

Keep in mind that this is not a comprehensive list and that experiencing one or some of the above characteristics does not necessarily mean one has low resilience. The combination of these factors, though, could indicate the condition. One of the most important things to consider about building resilience is that it's often difficult to discover an individual path to improved resilience. As such, keeping an open mind to accepting help from others is fundamental; be willing to reach out to supportive individuals.

A very timely and global example of resilience has occurred recently, with millions of people working in vastly different jobs. Pandemic-related relocation of workers from standard workplaces to home offices gave people time to reflect on their careers. There was even more time to reflect, in those cases where people either lost their jobs or were temporarily laid-off due to the pandemic. For the first time in their careers, many began questioning if their job, occupation or profession was a good fit for them.

As a result, many workers have viewed the pandemic as a turning-point; an opportunity to reinvent themselves and to plan a path to a far more rewarding and satisfying job or occupation. In numbers rarely seen in the last century, there has recently been a mass exodus of workers at all rungs up and down the ladder, from unskilled labor minimum-wage type jobs to highly skilled, handsomely paid jobs. Although this is putting some pressure on employers, supply chains and the economy, it's a great example of resilience. Individuals are examining ways in which their careers could be better and making the courageous decision to forge ahead in a new direction; some are doing this far later in their careers than they would ever have imagined.

Sometimes resilience is defined by how we bounce back from a bad event, but in other instances, such as the mass career shift just mentioned, it has more to do with an individual coming to the conclusion that things could be better; they bounce from what they suddenly realize has been an ongoing, unsatisfactory situation to something that could be far better. In the case of people migrating to new career roles, the pandemic was an opportunity to awaken from a deep and restless sleep. When they opened their eyes, many workers saw that their job, workplace or occupation was either not meeting their basic needs or was making them miserable. Some of the more common reasons people gave for wanting to make a career change included low wages or just not being able to pay the bills, abusive bosses or coworkers, toxic environments (socially and environmentally), monotonous responsibilities, unrealistic expectations that created unmanageable stress, lack of respect and dignity from superiors, and roles that were completely incongruent to their own profile.

Other workers who chose to move in a new career direction had been struggling with employer policies or procedures, particularly those involving clients, in which dishonesty, unethical practices or placing profit over human welfare were commonplace and expected. These people realized that even though they were merely soldiers following orders, the dishonorable practices that they were forced to follow, were slowly killing them on the inside. Another cluster of job hoppers were frustrated with the lack of potential or room for growth; these individuals felt that they were wasting their lives and that they could do so much more.

For many of these people, the bad career fit began as a temporary job that they just never left. For others, their career path was poorly planned. Yet others realized that their own needs and desires had changed significantly over the years, rendering the previously satisfying job much less desirable. There were other situations in which an employer or role changed so drastically over the course of one's career, that it no longer checked any of the employee's boxes.

As negative as the pandemic was, it provided the catalyst that these people needed to actually consider and then act on doing something better. It took something large and disruptive to kick-start their resilience. The important thing was, and still is, that rather than dwelling on how unpleasant things were, they made the choice to do the work that's required to improve their situation.

 Suddenly coming to the realization that a career change was due, many of these disenchanted employees immediately began looking for new opportunities that allowed them to move laterally to a new employer that offered a better fit and, in some cases, a far better compensation package.

Others realized that a complete career overhaul was required. They made a conscious decision to do it right; they took the time to do some deep introspection about their own needs, desires and values as they pertain to career, and they properly and carefully explored the types of jobs, occupations or professions that would best fit. Unlike the proverbial rock star wannabe teenager with zero musical ability or talent, these folks looked at options that accurately fit their skills, interests, values and desires. They also explored the reality of the job market to ensure that their new path would be in demand now and into the foreseeable future.

So many people work in roles or for companies that they dislike. Each year, several different surveys of American workers reveal interesting and sometimes shocking statistics regarding job satisfaction. While the different studies and surveys rarely come to the same statistical conclusions, many of them that were conducted over the last 10 years suggest that a majority of Americans are either somewhat or very dissatisfied with their jobs. In most of these cases, workers stay put. Why? Quite simply, because they are stuck. Personal and family circumstances often make leaving or switching jobs unfeasible. You know what this is all about if you've ever been there. This represents a type of resilience that's rarely talked about.

Taking a chance on anything, whether it be a career change or just about anything else, involves risk. Heck, living life involves risk! But sometimes, taking the chance isn't worth the potential downside of that risk. In spite of feeling stuck in their career, but also knowing they can't afford to take the financial risk, the change in schedule or the potential loss of another circumstance that binds them to their current employment, some people still wake every morning with a smile, motivated to get back to work. Now that's resilience!

The point is that resilience can be shown in different and sometimes opposing ways. While one person drums up the courage to completely revamp their career to do something that they're passionate about, someone else makes the

sacrifice for family and plods on, trying to find passion in what they do. Both of these people have shown brilliant resilience!

Although some people are more resilient than others, it doesn't mean that low resilience can't be improved. Psychological resilience and physical resilience are both pliable; the truth is that we can become more elastic to bounce back better and faster. Sometimes, though, it seems like resilience is set in stone. When we talk about physical resilience, for example, someone who was born with high immunity rarely gets colds and viruses, and tends to heal very quickly from illnesses, injuries and even surgery. We all know people like this and sometimes we envy them. We might muse, "Why did they get the good immunity stuff and I'm stuck with the leftovers that make me so vulnerable to colds and other illnesses? I always feel like a big infection sponge!"

It's true that genetics have a lot to do with one's physical resilience. Genetics determine predisposition to a lot of things and physical resilience is one of those things. But what would you say if you could override that particular genetic code? Even though your physical bounce-back may be weak, it doesn't have to stay that way.

One of the best ways to build up your physical resilience is to improve your emotional resilience, because the two are connected. Changing your thinking habits and improving your psychological self can have a dramatic effect on improving not only your emotional resilience, but also your physical resilience. Chronically depressed and anxious people, those who have lost hope and who have no vision for a good future, and those who feel trapped, have a negative impact on their physical immunity, which affects their physical resilience.

Other things that can help one become

more physically hardy are as follows:

● **Introduce a Healthier Diet.** Focus on fresh vegetables and fruits, whole grains and healthy proteins. Unless you are a vegan or are committed to a plant-based diet, meat is not your enemy; after all, meat has been a staple and important part of our diet as human beings for hundreds of thousands of years. As noted previously in Toolbox #2 (Treating Your Body Well), the key is in balance and moderation. Too much of any one thing (or too much of a lot of things) is not good. Meats, wild-caught fish, poultry, dairy, eggs, seeds, nuts, pulses (beans and lentils) and certain grains such as quinoa are great sources of protein. Fiber is also essential for a variety of reasons.

● **Throw Out the Unhealthy Foods.** Avoid anything that has been overly processed. If it comes from a box, needs to be re-constituted or is a packaged ready-to-eat dinner, it's not necessarily bad for you, but it very well could be. Learn how to read the nutrition panel on packaged foods and learn what the ingredients are. Avoid processed foods that are high in sodium (salt), sugars, nitrates, nitrites, saturated fats, and unnecessary chemicals and preservatives. There's nothing wrong with fast food every once in a while, but a consistent diet of drive through burgers and fries, pizza, wings, fried chicken…you get the idea.

● **Get Physical.** As noted elsewhere in this book, regular exercise is an important part of mental and physical health. It is also particularly important when it comes to mental and physical resilience. If you've let yourself go and haven't exercised in a long time, get a medical assessment before you launch a "new you" and start a fitness regimen. If you're planning to attend a gym, invest in yourself and use the add-on services of a certified trainer. Another thing to consider is that many people set such high goals when they start exercising on their own, that they are virtually impossible to sustain. Start slow and steady. Build as your body is able to take greater amounts of physical stress. Even a daily 15-minute walk is far better for you than none at all. *(Always consult your physician before starting an exercise program.)*

Consider this; Brent starts out with a 15 or 20 minute daily walk that he can complete every day for a few weeks, graduating to more strenuous or lengthy activity in the coming weeks. By the end of the first month, he's lost some weight, is a lot more flexible and feels great. However, Melissa sets an unattainable goal of a two hour walk on the very first day, but is way too sore the next day to do anything physical. Her ultimate goal of running for an hour by the end of two weeks never comes to fruition. Avoid setting unattainable goals. Slow and steady with incremental gains will always win.

• **Find More Active Ways of Doing Sedentary Things.** It would be just too easy to tell you to put away your phone, ditch the tablet, put down the book or stop watching TV. Although this book advocates limitation of screen time, it's unreasonable to stop it entirely. You're not going to give up using and doing these things, nor should you, because even if you did, it wouldn't last very long.

Alternatively, think of ways that you can make the typically sedentary parts of your life more active. Get on a treadmill while you watch your favorite episode of that series you're secretly addicted to! Listen to an audio book while you walk or run, rather than curling up on the sofa to read one. Try standing while you do things that you might normally do while seated. Whether you work from home or at an office, consider getting or enquiring about a convertible standing/sitting work desk. Before you stumble out of bed in the morning, establish a healthy stretching routine to get blood flowing to the muscles and to your brain. *(*This last tip also yields surprisingly effective and rapid results in terms of feeling more energetic and pain-free as you start your morning routine.)*

● **Stop Putting Poisons into Your Body.** This one sounds obvious; why would anyone poison themselves? Perhaps they're not aware of it. Workplace guidelines for hazardous materials in North America are defined by the Occupational Safety and Health Administration (OSHA) in the U.S. and by the Workplace Hazardous Materials Information System (WHMIS) in Canada. Both define routes of entry for hazardous substances entering the body, as being through inhalation, ingestion, absorption and injection. The fact is, we put a variety of hazardous things into our bodies in these ways.

Smoking and vaping are two of the most common ways we *inhale* poisons into our bodies. Vaping nicotine removes the hazardous smoke, but keep in mind that nicotine itself is defined by the Environmental Protection Agency (EPA) as an **acute hazardous waste**! It is highly addictive and causes high blood pressure, narrowing of the arteries, heart disease and other illnesses. When we smoke tobacco it's even worse; we not only inhale nicotine, but also **thousands** of other chemicals, many of which are carcinogenic (they cause cancer). Spray painting furniture or other items without a proper mask, even indoors without proper ventilation is another common way we inhale poisons.

We also *ingest* a lot of poisons. Beyond the unhealthy food choices mentioned earlier, we also routinely ingest toxic chemicals like alcohol and caffeine. Keep in mind that, as with other hazardous chemicals, the *amount* determines the danger. Some chemicals are necessary to live, such as water. However, even water can kill us if we drink too much of it at one time. Everyone knows that drinking too much alcohol can impact our health negatively, such as liver disease, as well as the risk of alcoholism since it is an addictive chemical. While previous studies suggested that one or two glasses of wine daily may contribute to some people's health, increasing amounts beyond that threshold can have negative impacts on various body systems and organs. Similarly, a cup or two of coffee or tea daily can be good for some people, but in the same way, increasing amounts beyond that may cause ill health.

In terms of **absorption** of toxins, we may not be aware that some of the things that we slather onto our skin are actually poisonous. Some brands of older sunscreen, for example, contain benzene, which is a potent carcinogen. Spraying or spreading certain common pesticides, herbicides and fertilizers on the lawn and garden can lead to absorption of dangerous poisons if we neglect to follow proper precautions, including the use of PPE such as gloves, respirators, goggles and long pants/long sleeved shirts. (Use of many of these types of chemicals also carries other risks to environment and water supply.) Many brands of hair dyes, skin moisturizers, cosmetics, fragrances, deodorants, antiperspirants and other toiletries contain toxins which absorb very efficiently through the skin and into the bloodstream. Check labels and, when possible, choose organic or *genuinely* natural toiletries, lotions and cosmetic products.

When it comes to improving your **psychological or emotional resilience**, keep in mind that there is a symbiotic relationship, with exercise being in the middle, and physical resilience and psychological resilience on either side. Visualize a Venn diagram with three circles; the circle on the left represents physical resilience, the center one is for exercise and the one on the right is for emotional or psychological resilience. Each of the left and right circles overlap the middle one evenly. In other words, exercise has a positive impact on both types of resilience. Additionally, improving physical resilience increases your emotional resilience and, likewise, improving your emotional resilience increases your immunity, which, in turn, increases your physical resilience. **This is an awesome 3-way causal relationship wherein physical resilience, exercise and psychological resilience are all connected.**

With a focus on the psychological side, your emotional resilience is less genetically determined than the physical side. However, they can both be improved regardless of genetics. Emotional resilience, though, is more of a learned skill. For instance, what type of resilience role modeling did you observe while growing up? If your parent frequently crumbled into pieces, rather than bouncing back from disappointments, trauma or bad circumstances, you likely learned this and that harmful pattern was imprinted on your own resilience. If you never learnt coping skills and didn't get to observe a parent's feisty desire to recover quickly from undesirable things, you simply never learned some very important life skills.

Beyond physical exercise, there are several other things you can try integrating into your daily life that will help you become more emotionally elastic. Here they are:

• **Understand that Resilience Comes with Pain.** Even the most resilient people experience distress, upset and a host of difficult emotions when faced with trauma or significantly undesirable circumstances. It's part of life. You can't expect the hurt to go away immediately and/or completely just because you are resilient. Resilient people, just like those who are not very resilient, experience negative emotions; sometimes quite intensely, depending on the severity of the circumstances or trauma. However, the difference is that they are better equipped to get on with life and often do so much more quickly.

• **Change Your Circumstances if You Can; If You Can't, then Accept them.** Sticking your head in the sand and just wanting things to go back to the way they were, is about as effective as expecting your bills to continue being paid after losing your job. It just doesn't work that way. A key step in becoming resilient is to have courage and make the effort to change what is changeable. Resilient people do not allow negative circumstances to have the last word if there is *any* path to improvement. They also know when to accept those circumstances if they can't be changed, and then work on a plan to better live with the new situation.

• **Cultivate and Maintain Relationships.** A big part of resilience rests in maintaining social contact and taking advantage of the support that other people can provide. Becoming a loner when things go wrong is about the worst thing you can do. The social isolation of the pandemic has continued for many people, despite the fact that most things have opened-up and have allowed for more social freedom.

- **Become a Hope Magnet.** Surround yourself with positive stories and examples of real-life people who bounced back from trauma or unfortunate circumstances. If this is too upsetting, then look for other things that bring hope and positivity. CHOOSE to avoid reading, watching or listening to news or information that is depressing or hopeless. Instead, CHOOSE to bask in the glow of activities that bring you healing, joy and the desire to dream.

- **Explore IF this is a Good Turning-Point in Your Life.** Is it possible that, prior to your negative experience or circumstance, life wasn't all that great and could have been a lot better? We tend to look back at our past with rose-colored glasses, blocking-out all of the negativity that we experienced previously. It's referred to as the "Good Old Days" effect. Maybe change has been knocking at your door for a long time. It's entirely plausible that there are aspects of your life that have simply run their course; things that need change in order for you to be happier, to bring back that spark, to be self-actualized. Use your circumstance to reinvent yourself.

- **Keep Things in Perspective.** People with low resilience tend to get mired in a deep, thick mud of despair that's often way out of proportion to the actual circumstance. Find your inner-courage to face the facts for what they are. The monster grows bigger and scarier the longer we avoid looking at it. Another way of looking at it is that things always seem bigger until you get closer to them. From a distance, hills and bridges can look absolutely terrifying.

As we approach them, our perspective changes and they appear less and less intimidating.

Ultimately, resilience is something that is in your hands. You can choose to improve your own personal physical and emotional resilience, and invest the work that is required to get there. Or not; it's your choice. However, it's important to understand that complaining about how bad things are and continuing to wallow in that muck, without either making a change or accepting what you can't change and moving forward, is a really bad decision.

Life is a precious gift. Choosing to move on, to move ahead and to live life is a far better option, because there comes a point at which one no longer has the option. Regret is a horrible thing.

Chapter 8
"Is Our World Really that Fragile?

The world feels like a much more fragile place than it seemed before the pandemic, doesn't it? If you think about it, most people living today in North America and in parts of other G20 nations *(the nations with emerging or the most advanced economies)* enjoy economic privilege and/or opportunity that citizens of many other countries cannot even imagine. With the exception of those who are very advanced in years, throughout our entire lives, most members of the "G20 crowd" share something else beyond economic advantage; we have never experienced anything as world-altering as the pandemic.

Then you have the others; for nearly 1 billion people, the pandemic was nothing nearly as frightening as the daily misery that they have endured chronically from events such as famine, war and civil unrest. People living in those circumstances may have never felt that the world was all that indestructible due to their experience; for them, it was destructing continually. However, for the G20 crew, this feeling is something completely new, extremely worrisome and global. When you look at it in those terms, it's no wonder so many people are finding it difficult to return to an emotional state in which everything feels normal again.

This feeling that the world is suddenly far less stable is, in part, attributable to the pandemic. The feeling may also be partially due to bad timing. Although it's not a direct result of the pandemic, our free society doesn't seem quite as socially stable or politically harmonious and democratic as it did just 5 years ago. People around us seem far more impatient, short-tempered and even angry. We see and hear extreme and sometimes tragic examples of this regularly on the evening news; the incidence of road rage, of guns being discharged and punches being thrown over trivial disagreements has risen dramatically. People seem to be at odds with one another more than ever before, and appear to have lost their tolerance and ability to resolve disagreements civilly. It's hard to feel good about the world around us when we're constantly reminded about how different we are and how much the other side dislikes us. It's even worse when we're convinced by hate-peddling politicians, anti-establishment bloggers and pro-conspiracy media hosts that the other side is our mortal enemy.

Another thing that may feel novel to many is the previously unimaginable concept of losing our democracy and our privileged place in the world. With recent attempts to squash voting rights and other blatant attacks on the democratic process, the inconceivable has become a very real potential.

If we're completely honest with ourselves, for most of our lives it's been easy to shrug off the big stuff that occurred elsewhere in the world. It was easy for many to think, "Stories of civil unrest, juntas, dictators seizing power, famines, authoritarian regimes abusing citizens' civil rights and economies faltering to the point of full collapse; these things are part of this world, but they're not part of my world".

There used to be a blanket of psychological insulation – a mental force field of sorts – protecting "us" from those awful things. Selfishly comforting thoughts of, "That's so far from me and my life," and "That's awful for those people, but it could never happen here," or "It's so tragic, but they never seem to want peace," helped us bury the real, but, hidden fact that it really doesn't take much for things like this to happen in our own backyard.

The reality is that our world *IS* fragile; the potential for bad things to happen has always been there. We are likely more aware of it now due to the pandemic, the growing social and political divide and, as just mentioned, our increasingly fragile democracy. If your view of the world has changed since the pandemic and you believe that it is a far more fragile place, it may be comforting to realize that, in the long term, nothing has really changed. The worst of this pandemic may be in sight, despite the emergence of new variants; time will tell. Depending on when you're reading this, it may already be a thing of the past. There have been other pandemics and plagues throughout history, and they, too, came and went. The world went on in spite of them. Yes, there will likely be other pandemics in the future caused by other viruses and those, too, will come and go. As our future becomes our past, and our medical knowledge and capability increase in step, we will be able to combat future outbreaks with greater speed and efficacy.

To come to terms with the concept that the world is, truly, a fragile place is not necessarily a bad thing. As mentioned earlier, we in the G20 crowd have cocooned ourselves by manufacturing a mental distance between ourselves and others in the world to whom bad things happen. However, we've always known - at least buried deep in our minds – that those disasters and loss of freedoms could happen to anyone - yes, even to us! It's not anything that anyone, other than tyrants, would wish for, but things can happen in our world that can change our lives dramatically. It may be a healthy change in our thinking. Why, you may ask? Because, when we accept that reality, it can have two positive impacts.

First, it can be freeing in a sense to remove restrictions and obstacles that we have placed in front of ourselves. When we consider that our freedom, our good health, our economic prosperity and other privileges are not guaranteed, it may also encourage us to better appreciate these blessings! It's not just the world that is fragile; life, in general, is fragile. That may sound a bit pessimistic, but it's really not. The realization of this reality can result in one living one's life more fully. We are blessed and we are privileged. The blessing of life by itself is not permanent. At some point, we *will* reach our end of days; that is one reality of which everyone can be certain. Rather than worrying about when that last day will be or whether the world has another whammy to throw at civilization as it did with Covid is not only a useless waste of time, it's also counterproductive. It ends-up wasting the precious here and now.

It comes down to a choice. If you knew you had five years left on your ticket and had the good health to enjoy them, would you waste those 1,824 days mired in worry and gloom or would you live every one of those days to the maximum? Nobody can make guarantees about this world, but there's one thing that is certain. Whatever days you waste are gone forever.

The second positive impact of this broadened perspective on the fragility of our world has to do with **Healing the Divide**. This systemic feeling of "THEM VS US" that has ravaged our society is antithetical to peace and harmony. It is also experienced both on a macro as well as a micro scale. In other words, society reflects it, while we also feel and live it in our personal lives. Although we've been conditioned to regard the other side as our *enemy*, it's so important that you try to see beyond this hate-filled notion. To consider our fellow citizen *(or on a global scale, our fellow human being)* an enemy just because they have beliefs and/or opinions that diverge from our own, is absolutely preposterous! It's not in our human nature to see others in such a polarizing manner, but it is something that has been fed to us; particularly during the last five years.

Regrettably, Covid has also thrown a wedge of division into long-standing friendships and even families. I'm willing to bet that you know of a situation with a friend or family member that reflects the following personal stories; stories that have played out in so many of our personal and family relationships. Linda is planning to attend her nephew's wedding, but later decides to decline the invitation when she learns that some of the bridal party and guests are not vaccinated. She's devastated, because she's so close to her nephew but with her age and medical condition, can't take the chance. She's now also heartbroken, because her sister and nephew have said horrible things about her due to her decision not to attend.

Here's another familiar narrative; family dinner at the Thomson's used to be a highlight of the week, sort of like Sunday dinner at the Reagan's on the popular CBS television series "Blue Bloods". However, unlike the Reagan's, the Thomson's weekly dinners were broken-up by earlier Covid restrictions. Once this large family was allowed to dine together in one place, the memories of harmonious dinners were quickly forgotten due to the fury and division between family members who were at odds with each other over combative philosophies regarding masking, vaccination and political culture. As we break free from the pandemic, perhaps there is hope for these paused relationships. People just need to remember how much these relationships added to their enjoyment of life.

Another indicator of the growing societal divide has to do with populism. Populism in politics around the world is nothing new, but in the past few years, it has reared its ugly head with greater fervor. This type of political ideology tends to pit people with different political affiliations against one another. It pushes people to believe that their party represents the views of almost everyone, while followers of the other party are mortal enemies.

In this scenario, instead of working collaboratively for the good of all, which ultimately produces the greatest positive progress, political issues never get resolved and rifts grow wider. All the while, solutions and support for important needs are not met. If there is a kernel of positivity to any of this, it's that, perhaps it's made us aware of the fragility of our world, and has given us an understanding of how rapidly a free society can descend into chaos, authoritarianism and civil unrest. Awareness of this potential is CRUCIAL to stop it from happening. Over history, many successful nations were forged **after** bloody wars and civil unrest took a horrible human toll. However, those new nations that sprouted from the ashes could only grow and become successful by focusing on healing and opportunities for **everyone,** and by finding common good. No nation was ever built on divisiveness. Division kills democracy. Division kills opportunity. Division kills freedom. Division kills economic progress. These scary lessons should be reinforced. Similarly, we need to hear more about how coming together, despite our differences, is the only thing that secures opportunity, freedom and prosperity.

The Latin words *"Communis"* and *"Communicare"* are related to the concepts of finding things in common, sharing and bringing together. Although you can't do it alone, your contribution to these ancient principles is a way in which you can help change the world. Finding the good in your fellow person, regardless of their political, philosophical, cultural or religious beliefs, will help heal our post-pandemic world and has the wonderful bonus of helping you to heal yourself.

Your fellow countryperson, your fellow *human*, is not your enemy. Try to see people who are on the other end of your philosophical spectrum through a different lens. Ask why they feel the way they feel or why they may believe what they believe. Don't ask these questions with a view to convincing them that you are correct and they are not. They may not be right, according to your beliefs or opinions, but if we are to preserve freedom, it means that different voices, cultures, political slants, religions and mindsets all have a place.

In conversation or contact, when you are open-minded and tolerant of someone with opposing views rather than being judgmental, angry or belligerent, something quite surprising happens. Some of their tough veneer begins to soften. They start to view you as less of an enemy or threat and more as a fellow human being with a different mindset. They even begin to understand your point of view and, while they probably won't change theirs, may start to ask some objective questions about both sides of the split. We learned it in kindergarten; it's called "getting along."

You see, in the end, if we treat our fellow person as an enemy, it really means that we want that person defeated. While we may succeed in winning, unfortunately in the process, we also kill off the spirit of peace, harmony, hope and freedom.

Our politicians could really benefit from this type of epiphany, don't you think?

Stephen J. Kristof

Chapter 9

Retiring During Covid

This chapter will resonate particularly well with individuals who retired during the pandemic and who struggled with the adjustment to retired life more intensely and for longer than they expected. Indeed, many people may still be experiencing that struggle. If this describes your situation, this chapter may also answer many of the questions you've been wondering about since you pulled the plug from work. If you are planning to retire *soon* or you retired *prior* to the pandemic, but found the transition to be difficult, you'll likely gain some helpful insight.

Retirement is often referred to as the "next chapter of your life." It's interesting, almost humorous, how "Happy Retirement" greeting cards frequently feature images of palm trees, hammocks, beach scenes, Adirondack chairs and cruise ships. If only it were that simple and carefree! Whether you retired following a long-term commitment to a single employer, like many of our ancestors did, or you climbed the career ladder while moving from job-to-job and from one company to the next, the reality is that once you retire, you have a new job that you may not have expected. More on that in a bit…

Fortunately, many new retirees slide into their new lives smoothly, without regret and without a care; so carefree, in fact, that they never look back. That's how it's *supposed* to work. Heck, we spend anywhere from 30 to 50 or more years working our butts off and it sure seems like after paying our dues for so long, we deserve to reap the fruits of our labor; that is, to enjoy a stress-free, long and healthy retirement! Unfortunately, it doesn't always work that way and the transition itself can be far more difficult than many expect.

The reasons why the transition from work life to retirement can be so challenging for so many people are rather complex. Priorities a person assigned to their career and to their life outside of work while they were working influence their ability to adjust to retired life. Other things that influence the adjustment include social status or power that the job or career represent, one's financial security upon retirement, post-retirement pension or future income stream, how much one likes the job and how much happiness one derives from daily contact with colleagues. Being emotionally prepared for retirement also impacts the ease of transition. Finally, having a plan and expectations for post-retirement living also has a big impact. All of these things will dictate how smooth or difficult that transition may be.

I very recently had a conversation with an out-of-town acquaintance whom I met several years ago. Up until his retirement a few months prior, he was the police chief of a mid- to-large sized Southwest city. Let's call him "James," although, of course, that's not his real name. I had some out-of-town business to attend in his area and, as fate would have it, I ran into him while picking-up dinner. Initially, he had no idea who I was, which I attributed to the mask covering my face and the fact that he didn't know I was in town.

We were in a parking lot at the time, so I removed my mask and asked, "So, how's retirement treating you?"

He finally recognized me. After expressing how surprised and happy he was to see me, we exchanged pleasantries and then I asked the question again. "How do you like being retired?"

James furled his left eyebrow, thought about it for a moment, and said while nodding his head up and down, "Well, it's *interesting*."

I asked, "What do you mean? How so?"

James said, "Now, don't get me wrong; I'm really enjoying it. But it's been a bit harder to get to where I want to be than I expected. It's the emotional stuff that can throw you."

Again, I asked him to explain. James continued, "So, keep in mind that as a Police Chief, there's an enormous degree of responsibility; I lived and carried my job with me everywhere I went, whether I was in my office, meeting with the mayor, out to dinner with my wife and even while sleeping. It wasn't unusual for me to be abruptly stirred from a deep sleep at 3 in the morning because the media wanted a comment about an emergency or controversial incident that I hadn't even been aware had occurred! I never stopped being the Chief of Police for the past many years."

I said, "That sounds very exciting and very exhausting at the same time."

James said, "Exactly. I really thrived on the challenges, but there's no doubt it was wearing me down. You know, when you are essentially the "buck-stops-here guy" for law enforcement and for keeping the peace in a large community, every little decision you make is a weighty one." James continued, "I've got the mayor crawling down my back one minute, the FBI liaising with me about terrorism preparedness and, then, rank-and-file discipline is always around the corner."

As I listened, I tried to imagine what his life had been like and I began to feel overwhelmed just thinking about it. I asked, "So what was it like stepping away from all of that? It must have been like a huge rush of relief, huh?"

James smirked, saying, "Well, my last official day of work was on a Friday. There was the usual hoopla, along with well-wishes and what you'd expect. That night, my wife threw a big retirement party and it was a blast; lots of colleagues, friends and relatives," he paused for a moment and looked upward, then looked back at me and continued, "and then it was all over."

He continued, saying, "I woke up fairly early the next day. I arranged for my last day of work to be on a Friday, because Saturday has always been my favorite day of the week and I had looked forward to my first day of freedom being on a Saturday! I had my coffee and read the paper."

He continued, saying, "Then, like the cat that ate the canary, I smiled and chuckled. I realized that I could do whatever I wanted and could do it on my OWN schedule. I decided to wash the SUV. I stood there wearing shorts and an old t-shirt, sponge in hand and then it hit me like a ton of bricks. All of a sudden, I was just a regular guy washing his car in the driveway."

James went on to explain how he was terribly unprepared for the realization that, in an instant, his professional status, importance in the community, prominence in tackling huge problems and all of the stature that comes along with it, had disappeared into thin air. While he was looking forward to dropping the stress of tackling huge problems that had no easy solution, he ignored the fact that he derived a great deal of pleasure and prestige from the other aspects of his job. To a certain extent, a good chunk of his self-image was tangled up with his job, so when he did finally retire, he wasn't sure what was left. As he put it, "Even though I was standing on the same spot on my driveway that I had stood on thousands of times before, somehow, my footing was different."

It generally goes this way; the more career-related authority, responsibility and social status one has prior to retiring, the more difficult it is fitting into a "regular life" after retirement. The problem is compounded when the individual fails to cultivate a life outside of work. When family, social friends, pastimes, personal interests, spirituality and personal needs take a back seat to career – or worse yet, when they are sacrificed for the sake of career – the void upon retirement can feel like a deep pit of despair.

The problem also occurs when one confuses a sense of self with one's career. It occurs frequently; people derive their identity and sense of self-worth from career-related importance and status. Once that work is over, what's left? Suddenly, the newly minted retiree no longer feels important, relevant or valued. He or she struggles with a crashing sense of doubt because of leaving their job and experiences feelings of powerlessness.

Regrettably, some people don't realize how important the non-work side of their lives has always been until they finally pull the plug on their career. Then there are those who, I guess, plan to work forever. They like to give an ominous kernel of advice to anyone contemplating retirement. It goes something like this, "As soon as you retire, you're on a fast-track to death."

Well, that's scary advice; especially for people who have enjoyed a long and satisfying work life, and who are looking forward to enjoying the rest of their life! What's even more frightening is that various peer-reviewed studies have shown that people who retire at the age of 55 are significantly more likely to die earlier in the 10 years following retirement than those who retire at 65. If you've recently retired or are about to and you are younger than 65, don't despair! A more recent German study conducted in 2009 had the opposite conclusion. Those who retired early, actually lived *longer* than those who retired later in life.[xxv] That study took into consideration mitigating factors such as the fact that unhealthy people are more likely to retire sooner than healthy people.

The bottom line is that retirement can and routinely does cast some people into some very deep, dark and lonely waters. The self-doubt and lingering feeling that one has no purpose in life can crush one's spirit and often pushes recent retirees into some form of depression. As noted earlier, the negative emotions such as feeling like one has less authority, relevance, importance and status impact self-esteem. So often, busy employees nearing retirement lament the fact that they have no time for themselves, only to discover after retiring that they don't know what to do with all of that time.

It can be a difficult time, even for those who worked hard at cultivating the non-work side of their lives and who developed a plan for retired life. They may find that their newfound freedom feels strange for the first few months up to a year or even longer. The complaint is often that things just don't feel or seem normal. (It sounds a lot like what we've been hearing about the pandemic.) The departure from normality is felt at a far deeper level for those who wrapped themselves up too tightly in their careers.

The pandemic compounded the stress and lack of normality that commonly accompany retirement.

This is where it gets interesting. Even though many people can expect to experience a temporary aura of strangeness upon retirement, what happens when that coincided with the feeling of a lack of normality from the pandemic? The result is a far more intense sense that something is wrong in one's life and in the world. According to the American Association of Retired Persons (AARP), the pandemic forced millions of workers to retire earlier than expected.[xxvi] This means that many of those workers had not yet reached the level of financial preparedness or security that they may have intended to have upon retirement, which is an added stress in one's transition to retired life. It also means that many of those early retirees were also not mentally prepared to make the jump.

All in all, it was a perfect storm for countless retirees. **For many, the adjustment was exacerbated by a lack of financial and mental preparedness due to an unexpectedly early retirement forced by the pandemic, on top of the pandemic's own cruel brand of abnormality.**

This insight may be particularly valuable if you, as a recent retiree, are wondering why it's been so difficult and is taking so long to feel normal again. In short, it may provide some reassurance that there's nothing wrong with you; it's just that timing was really bad and that wasn't your fault. You are certainly not alone. While being in good company doesn't necessarily make the adjustment any easier, one at least realizes that he or she is not abnormal.

At times during my own career, I've helped clients in career and employment matters; for several years I managed a career counselling company that directly served employees from entry-level through to top executive status, occasionally also consulting with employees who were let go, through corporate outplacement contracts. At another point, I worked in a supervisory capacity as an employment consultant for a Fortune 500 company. While most of the clientele whom I served were in the midst of career advancement or were seeking a lateral placement, I also dealt with a fair share of clients who were transitioning from career to retired life. If I learned anything from these experiences, it was that adjusting to retirement involves a greater challenge than most people realize or expect. I would commonly hear comments like, "I thought I was prepared," or, "I don't feel useful anymore," and, "I feel an emptiness that my leisure activities don't seem to come close to filling."

It's so sad when someone puts so much effort, primacy and focus on their career, just to realize at the end of it, that although it was an important part of one's life, it was not the only important part. You see, while some experts say that you need a few years to properly prepare for retirement, in terms of preparing mentally for it, the honest truth is that it's closer to a 10-year process. Of course, preparing for the financial reality of one's post-retirement needs is something that should be at the *front-end* of one's career, but that's a completely different thing. For the purposes of this book, suffice it to say that people who only recently thought about retirement and were then thrust into the thick of it during the pandemic, had an awful lot to deal with.

When it comes to feelings of pride and self-image that intertwine with the career part of our lives, it's often one of the toughest things to deal with in retirement. In fact, you would be surprised how many recently retired prominent executive clients paid my company to have a professional resume crafted; I certainly was surprised by it.

So, why did a retired former owner of a funeral home chain, a retired real estate developer, a retired executive manager of a large multinational manufacturing plant – and many others – hire my company to create post-retirement resumes? I recall an 88-year-old, highly successful, former entrepreneur showing up for his appointment with his 65-year-old son in tow *(maybe the towing was the other way around)*. This prominent octogenarian never had or needed a resume throughout his career, but at his age, now wanted a personalized crystallization of his career path and accomplishments.

These dynamic, prominent and successful entrepreneurs and executives had no need for a resume, but they all wanted to pay for someone to create a comprehensive visual representation of their career path and achievements; ultimately, what they saw as their success in life. I realize it's an oversimplification, but the main thing that I learned from these experiences was that it's one thing to have pride and satisfaction in a career well played, but quite another thing to clutch shreds of that former career as it slips away, as if it defined one's self-worth and self-image.

<u>Obviously, there's a lesson here for people who are far from retirement</u>. It goes something like the old cliché-question that is often mistakenly attributed to Confucius; "Do you live to work or work to live?" Perhaps the right answer is a combination of both! If one lives to work, then one devotes most of one's finite hours on this earth to work and ignores the rest of what life has to offer. If one works to live, then one enjoys the richness of life, but may not be so satisfied with the work side of things.

The math reveals that working 8 hours per day, 5 days per week = 40 standard hours per week. If you remove a standard 3-week annual vacation period from the mix, the average employee will work 1,960 hours per year; during an average 35-year career, he or she will therefore work 68,600 hours. During those same 35 years, a human lives 306,600 hours. Thus, work takes-up about 22% of an average person's time during their working years.

For someone who devotes their life to work (the "live to work" crowd), work takes-up a far greater proportion of their time on this planet. When that work is done, what's left? What did that person cultivate outside of work that is also personally rewarding, valuable and satisfying?

It's been said that if you choose a job you love, you'll never have to work a day in your life (*another misappropriated quote that Confuclus never actually said*). Maybe this is why the best advice is to choose wisely in planning a career path that will allow you to really enjoy your work life – and – at the same time, cultivate a life outside of work that is rich and enjoyable. This way, one has the best of both worlds. He or she "works to live," so the primary priority is on life outside of work, but they still derive much pleasure from the work that they do. It's advice that I've given frequently to young adults planning a career. It's also advice that

I feel will make them happy during their working life and well after it.

Okay, this all makes a lot of sense, but it doesn't do anything to help you if you are struggling with a planned – or worse yet – unexpected retirement that coincided with the pandemic. The most obvious cause of the angst and feelings of abnormality of this unique circumstance is that **you left work and entered into a major life transition during a time of extreme stress, anxiety and uncertainty**. Even if you did have plans to begin doing, "What you want, where you want and when you want," (one of the most anticipated advantages of retirement), you may not have been able to take advantage of those plans, due to ongoing pandemic waves and Covid-related restrictions.

Upon retirement, many people hope to travel, vacation, and visit relatives and friends who live elsewhere. It's one of the most common expectations of retirement. However, it simply didn't happen under Covid. Some people are more comfortable with travel than others, but the fact is that many people are still reticent when it comes to air travel, boarding a cruise ship, staying in hotels or at resorts, dining out and a host of other things that are involved in travel and vacations. It is an awfully big disappointment to plan for and look forward to this type of freedom upon retirement, only to be basically stuck at home waiting for the pandemic to eventually pass.

Of course, because pretty much everything in our lives was altered in some way due to Covid, and some changes are still ongoing, even if we had cultivated a rich assortment of interests, hobbies, recreation and activities to help fill the void, many of those types of things were either temporarily halted or have slipped away.

Here are some helpful tips if you continue to experience difficulty transitioning to retirement and feel that it may have been complicated by the pandemic.

1. Try to Mentally Separate the Newness of Retirement from the Abnormality of the Pandemic.
This seems obvious, but it's important to detach one from the other. The fact is that the degree to which you feel off and abnormal may have less to do with your new chapter in life than it does with the pandemic. The two things compound to create a worse state of mind than either one would by itself. You may actually be further along in your transition to retirement than you realize, but the continuing fallout and residue from the pandemic is making your progress difficult to discern.

2. Start Enjoying Things that You Expected to Enjoy.
Granted, you still may not be able to or don't yet feel comfortable taking that once-in-a-lifetime trip to some distant corner of the world, but there are other destinations and options that will have to do for now. At the time of this writing, travel around the globe continues to be iffy, with different countries experiencing widely varying rates of infection and hospitalization. Put the more exotic plans on hold and go to where you're able to safely go for now. Even though it may not be everything you expected, it will go a long way to helping kick-start your retirement into a more productive and enjoyable gear! It also doesn't need to be travel.

Think about the different things that you had planned to do upon retirement. Just because some of those things were shelved, doesn't mean you can't do them now. You may need to make temporary adjustments, but the fact is that life isn't waiting around for you, so grab what you can.

3. Fill Your Days with People.
Establish a regular morning coffee arrangement with a friend or former coworker; particularly with someone else who has recently retired. If you have a spouse or a significant other in your life, plan everyday things together; going to a market, a neighborhood walk, hiking, any sport, visiting arts and culture venues, dining out, taking daytrips or any other activity that you both enjoy.

4. Who Needs Help? Be There For Them.
Whether it's a through a formal volunteer placement, an informal visit with a friend in need or being a helpful caregiver, helping others can go a very long way to improving our sense of relevance, self-worth and self-esteem. It also carries the benefit of making a positive difference. Obviously, we all have different skills, personality characteristics and interests, so make sure that you're not replacing an aspect of your old job that you disliked with a new activity that you hate! As a result, when choosing to volunteer or help others, consider donating your time and competence in ways that are encouraging, interesting, non-threatening and that you would look forward to engaging in.

5. Establish Routine and Schedules.
This is borrowed from some of the general advice in this book, but it has special significance when it comes to the newly retired. Don't expect to somehow automatically transition from regular routines and schedules to a life without them, without it feeling odd! It may initially seem brilliant and freeing to live without them, but most retirees begin to feel unproductive,

lethargic and down in the absence of some form of a timetable and customary activities.

6. Ask if You Would Rather be Working?

Whether your magic number finally came due or the pandemic forced your hand and retirement is now upon you, it does not mean that you can't be working again. For a lot of people, their initial retirement is quite brief, with some folks spending only a month or two before they find themselves back in the saddle. Are you really ready for retirement or do you miss work so much that you would be far happier doing something of a career sort once again? Only you can answer this question honestly, but if you continue to doubt your new situation and, despite trying different strategies, still yearn for work, it might be time to dust-off the old resume and seek out a position that will bring you new energy and determination.

A few caveats, though, if you plan to throw yourself back into a work situation; firstly, discuss your thoughts and plans with your spouse or partner if you have one in your life. Singlehandedly deciding to return to work can cause immeasurable damage to relationships in which the non-working spouse or partner is laser focused on spending remaining years together without the stress, distraction and inflexibility that returning to work often carry.

Second, be selective! You have already paid your dues and have done the dirty work. It's one thing if you need the extra income, but if not, look for something that is somehow related to the best and most enjoyable aspects of your former work. You don't want to be trading the boredom of retirement for drudgery.

Third, explore other unrelated opportunities that your former career did not allow. Choose part-time work over a full-time commitment. Consider a low-risk entrepreneurial project.

7. Learn Something New.

Time is on your side now! What do you want to know more about that you never had time to explore previously? Consider enrolling in a new course or program. Attend a seminar or workshop. "Audit" a university or college course that may be offered tuition-free for seniors or enroll in a full-out degree program if that's on your bucket list. Explore creative things that are educational, but also social and leisurely; take an art course, learn to play an instrument, try your hand at photography, take dance lessons, learn a new technology; the possibilities are endless!

8. (Wait a Year) and then Start a New Creative Project or Venture.

Most retirement experts advise their clients to enjoy everything their new life has to offer for a year before starting any major project or new venture. This does not work for everyone and only you will know when or if it's time to take on a formidable new challenge. That being said, when the time is right, consider directing some of your extra time to a new enterprise or endeavor that you've put off for years because your career prevented it.

In summary, retirement can be one of the most enjoyable phases in life, but it does take some adjustment. Keep in mind that the term retirement means different things to different people. The pandemic impacted all of us in different ways, but for recent retirees, it compounded what is often an already difficult transition. Explore where you're at and put some of the aforementioned advice into play if you are having a particularly rough time.

Stephen J. Kristof

Chapter 10
Believe in God

As the pandemic eventually winds down, global vaccination rates rise, successive waves become less threatening blips and variants are tamed, we will all finally be able to take a deep breath and reflect on where this experience has taken us, both as individuals and as a global community. Ultimately, we humans share far more likenesses than dissimilarities. One practice from which we can all benefit is that of contemplating how we have grown and/or changed, after having come through such a particularly challenging event in our lives.

So, how *have* you changed or grown from the overall challenge of this pandemic? You may not be there yet; hopefully this book offers some valuable perspectives to help you on your way to feeling more normal once again. However, whether you are already moving on with your life or have some more work to do, it really is an important question to think about. Now, please don't misinterpret this question as a suggestion that the pandemic was in any way a good thing; it was not. It was a very, very bad thing; it took the lives of at least 5 million people, isolated family and friends from one another, created upheaval, mayhem and distress wherever it landed, further divided nations and societies, and made hundreds of millions of people sick.

Having said this, there's nothing wrong with at least considering how we may be stronger, weaker or just different following the pandemic. This can provide helpful insight into areas of strength and areas that need further strengthening.

The next step requires thinking more broadly; not just globally, but even more broadly than that. Ask yourself how you fit into our universe. Bet you didn't expect that! Okay, it's a colossal leap, but answering this question could actually have a huge impact on the rest of your life. **Who are you in the universe?** What do you believe about why you are here in this life? **Do you realize that you are a sacred and unique soul, who was created with purpose, intention and divine power?** Or, sadly, have you convinced yourself that this life is nothing more than a scientific fluke and that you are but a blip that will come and go with the blink of an eye?

I cannot imagine believing the latter notion. To me, it sounds so frightening and lonesome; what a futile existence! If you consider yourself to be an atheist, agnostic or are just a spiritual cynic, you have the right to turn the page and move on. But, before you label me as a zealot whose main goal is to win you over, please understand that I respect your position. I don't agree with it, but I respect it, and I would only ask that you respect mine.

You see, one of the most precious aspects of living in a free society is to be able to exercise freedom of thought, of conscience and of religion. So, if you live in a nation that guarantees such freedoms, you have a very special privilege; many people in our world do not enjoy such fortune! While I do not understand why some people are born into such privilege while others are not, I know enough to feel gratitude. However, to whom shall I direct that gratitude? It's a fair question. I doubt that anyone would feel comfortable thanking themselves for such privilege.

The reason I broach the subject of divinity is due to the shift in perspective that the pandemic has created in many people. As noted earlier, the pandemic has made many people around the world question life itself. People who never previously thought about such things, now have doubts. **Having seen how a** microscopic pathogen could turn the world upside down and bring it to a halt, some people are now worried about how unforeseen events and other things in the future could diminish the blessings in life that they previously took for granted. As noted in Chapter 8, our world is fragile and many people have just realized that.

It has reminded us of our own responsibility in preserving the sanctity of life, harmony between people and the health of the earth. What we do with that insight is up to us. However, to fester on one's feelings of doubt and worry about stability of life on earth is both unproductive and counterproductive. There is one thing that can provide unparalleled peace of mind in this regard and that is, quite simply, our relationship with our Creator. **Faith creates hope and erases doubt.** This is precisely what the world needs at this time.

If you consider yourself to be a spiritual or "spirit-filled" individual, a logical question is, "How has your relationship with God been doing during the past few years of pandemic living?" The pandemic was difficult, but for many people, their connection with God provided the comfort of normality and peace of mind that far outpaced the help that other people and various strategies provided. That connection cultivated faith and hope and continues to do so.

The pandemic may have also led to your own questions about the relationship between God and your own healing. *To what extent, if any, does belief in a higher power have on healing, whether that healing be of a physical or psychological nature, or both?* Does prayer, spiritual meditation and one's relationship with God actually help people to heal? Or, is it just the belief itself that helps people to heal themselves? Is it possible that faith can generate a placebo effect, in that healing occurs because the believer thinks that prayer, rituals and one's spiritual relationship will have that positive effect? It's a fair question.

Multiple hundreds of peer-reviewed academic studies have been completed during the past few decades with similar hypotheses trying to prove or disprove the existence of a correlation between faith and healing. The studies were professionally designed and peer-reviewed, involving triple-blind, randomized, controlled trials aimed at ruling out mitigating factors. Despite the efforts, some studies reached opposite conclusions, while others left more questions than answers.

Nonetheless, the belief that there *is* a relationship between prayer and healing persists. As easily as this belief is brushed-off and even mocked by atheists, cynics and people who classify themselves as realists, there are far too many other people at this precise moment in time and in the timeline to this point, who believe that this relationship exists, because they or one of their loved ones actually experienced such healing. And then there are the countless physicians, surgeons and psychiatrists who have witnessed spontaneous remission in their patients' illnesses; prayerful patients with fervent faith.

A 2009 article in the Indian Journal of Psychiatry described the results of an objective review of several "faith and healing" themed academic trials and studies. The article's authors, Dr. Chittaranjan Andrade, M.D. [xxvii] and Dr. Rajiv Radhakrishnan, M.D.[xxviii] admitted that, disappointingly, randomized controlled studies on the efficacy of prayer on healing are basically futile because there are so many factors at play, that the relationship cannot be scientifically demonstrated one way or the other.

However, the authors also came to another, surprisingly rare conclusion. They wrote, "We must keep in mind that religion is based on faith and not on proof. This implies that, if God exists, he is indifferent to humanity or has chosen to obscure his presence. Either way, he would be unlikely to cooperate in scientific studies that seek to test his existence."[xxix]

The very essence of faith is trust in God without proof. If such proof existed, faith would be easy. Although faith in God is not easy, this much is true; faith is effective and real in helping people heal from physical and psychological illness. The ongoing plethora of examples that are unexplainable using any other reason cannot be ignored.

Dr. Harold G. Koenig, M.D., is a Professor of Psychiatry and Behavioral Sciences at Duke University School of Medicine. He has written and co-authored numerous books, articles and studies; some of them examining the relationship between faith and health. In his 2012 paper in the journal "ISRN Psychiatry", Dr. Koenig explored the relationship between religion and spirituality, and mental and physical health. [xxx] After reviewing *hundreds* of data-based research reports studying the relationship, Dr. Koenig came to the conclusion that the majority of those studies conveyed significant relationships between religion and spirituality, and better health.

There have been countless examples throughout history that illustrate the bond between faith, prayer and healing. Of course, some of them date back to biblical times, with accounts in both the Old and the New Testaments relating how faith and prayer led to divine miracles. However, we don't need to look that far back or very hard to find modern-day stories that bring hope to all.

Danielle Campo-McLeod is a world-class athlete, well-known in the international swimming circuit. Her story is one of inspiration and faith. When she was only 13, she broke four world records at the 1998 Paralympic World Champlonships in New Zealand. Two years later, the swimmer won 3 gold medals and a silver for her performance in her division at the 2000 Summer Paralympics in Sydney, Australia. In the following few years, Danielle went on to win even more gold and silver medals in other international Paralympic competitions. At the age of two, she was diagnosed with muscular dystrophy. Over the ensuing years, Danielle endured surgeries, ongoing pain and much difficulty completing everyday tasks due to her neuromuscular disease.

Her love of swimming started as a form of physiotherapy. Born in 1985, Danielle lived most of her life accepting that the pain and constant struggle would never go away. Muscular Dystrophy is, after all, one of those progressive, forever diseases. Despite the ongoing burden, she proved to the world that she was a world-class champion; people close to her already knew this.

It's amazing how quickly our lives can change. As a Director and Ambassador for Muscular Dystrophy Canada, she was fully immersed in the disease and its many challenges, but she never expected to learn what she did in the early summer of 2000. As the world struggled with how to navigate Covid-19, Danielle received exceptionally good news from her medical specialist. After 12 years of medical sleuth work, blood tests and genetic testing, Dr. Mark Tarnopolsky at McMaster University discovered that she had been misdiagnosed. He had finally pinpointed the genes that were responsible for her disease; Dr. Tarnopolsky determined that she had Congenital Myasthenic Syndrome, which is a neuromuscular condition that appears similar to Muscular Dystrophy. Of all of the types of neuromuscular diseases she could have, this one is the best, because it is treatable.

Shortly after the new diagnosis, Danielle was given two medications; Ephedrine, a drug that was formerly prescribed as a diet pill, but that is now used for other conditions including neuromuscular transmission, and Mestinon, a medication that increases the chemical responsible for communication between nerve impulses and muscle movement. Soon after taking her first dose, she was floored. After just two hours, she was ecstatic to find that her condition was improving. Danielle's life sentence was swiftly commuted. Prior to that, something as simple as opening a mayonnaise jar was difficult for her to do independently. Her beautiful new reality dawned on her as she opened a new jar by herself.[xxxi]

As the months passed, Danielle's symptoms all but disappeared; it was miraculous. By the end of the summer, she was telling local media that it was like having a brand-new body. Her story of courage and resilience is astounding; breaking multiple world records and earning medals at international competitions while living with a previously misdiagnosed, yet, debilitating disease revealed a fortitude most people can only imagine.

However, life is rarely so simple. Months after her new diagnosis and treatment, she became pregnant with a third child and was not able to take the new medications during her pregnancy. Her weakness and previous symptoms returned, but she pushed through. On August 17, 2021, Danielle gave birth to a daughter. Morgan would become the fifth child in Danielle and husband Denny's blended family. Sadly, complications followed the delivery and Danielle underwent several surgeries to correct a bowel obstruction. Pneumonia ensued. Less than a month after her daughter Morgan's birth, Danielle was back in hospital with septic shock, the most serious and final stage of sepsis, in which infection spreads through the blood and throughout the body.

"While Danielle struggled for her life in the ICU, her family fought for her using the most powerful medicine they knew; prayer."

By September Danielle was on life support in what would be the most crucial Olympic-level competition of her life. She was transported by air helicopter to the Critical Care Unit at Western

University Hospital, in London, Canada, where she clung to life, heavily sedated in an induced coma and on a ventilator. While Danielle struggled for her life in the ICU, her family fought for her using the most powerful medicine they knew; prayer.

Danielle's mother, Colleen, asked everyone to pray for her daughter. Colleen quickly started a *movement of prayer*, with the same intensity and determination that Danielle had earlier shown the world as an athlete. Colleen encouraged others to light candles as a symbol of prayer for her daughter's recovery. Local television, radio and newspaper media in Danielle's home region of Windsor, Ontario, helped get the word out, along with countless messages on social media. Her local church community also jumped on-board by encouraging members to pray for her and to light candles at church through the week.

The movement spread quickly. Danielle's husband, Denny, started receiving calls and messages from around the world. Those who knew Danielle personally weren't the only ones lighting candles and praying for her; people who only heard of her as well as complete strangers stepped up to the plate in response to her story. Prayers were pouring in for Danielle from her local community and from a truly global community.

As Danielle waited on death's doorstep, her family was gathered together three times by hospital staff, telling them there was nothing more that they could do. Despite the medical intervention and IV antibiotics, there were simply limits to earthbound efforts. However, the multitude of impassioned prayers may have done what medical efforts alone could not accomplish. Amazingly, Danielle's body began to overcome the infection; she regained consciousness and started to recover strength slowly, but, surely. By October 15, 2021, cat scans revealed that her infection was completely gone and she was returned to a local physical rehabilitation center. She was finally able to surprise her children with a return to home on Halloween.

Days after her return home, Danielle revealed during a television interview, that medical professionals could not believe that she was able to survive her level of infection.[xxxii] The fact that she was back home and healing after just a few months was nothing short of astonishing.

A few weeks after that interview, I had the opportunity to speak with Danielle.[xxxiii] She was continuing to work toward her full recovery, but explained that it takes time and tremendous effort. Danielle noted that most people don't realize how challenging it is to recover from something as serious as toxic shock leading to being on life support. However, it's clear that despite the pain of physiotherapy and other aspects along her road to recovery, Danielle is a fighter and will not stop until she reaches her goal.

I asked her to talk about her perspective on faith. She said with strong conviction, "It's the foundation of everything ...this is where you bring your struggles and not just your struggles, but you bring your successes as well. It's always been something that has just been taught by our parents as a part of everyday life."

Danielle, who has had more than her fair share of struggles, said that her faith has actually strengthened during the bad times. She also feels that gratitude is a huge part of faith. As she shared her take on faith, it became clear that Danielle's relationship with God is a very active and important priority in her life. For her, faith and connection are intertwined with her day-to-day life; not just the highlights. For example, when she was a child, her mother took her to church to get a blessing before her first international competition. The blessing was just as important to her as was the outcome of the competition. In terms of living her faith, she said, "It's not just at the end when you get the results, but through the whole process of it."

We talked about the events in her life during the year and a half leading up to her present-day recovery. When she took the new medications in the early summer of 2020 and experienced the astonishing and rapid turn-around in her decades-long neuromuscular condition, she said that it was incredible getting to experience what a strong body could feel like. After hitting the lowest physical point in her life, she now understands that it was necessary for her to have experienced the strength and lack of pain *before* she got toxic shock. She said, "I think it was a gift that this all happened in the order that it did, because I know how strong and how good this body can feel, so being able to go back to that was the motivation to kind of keep pushing for it in the hospital."

Another major thing that kept her motivated was her desire to be back at home with her family. She said that when she awoke from the coma and saw the tubes and medical apparatus, she had so many questions. However, she was not scared. That is the third thing that motivated her. She placed her faith in God, explaining that she had trust in the idea that, "His will be done."

Danielle's faith is one of beauty and courage. I asked her about how she reconciled the fact that, after enduring all of the challenges, surgeries and pain, she then ends up on life support, struggling to stay alive. She explained, "I've been through so many of these hard times now; maybe that's my 'Why'. God was preparing me this whole time to learn how to fight through those struggles in a body that hasn't been perfect, because now this is the biggest fight."

We explored her thoughts on the role that the candle and prayer movement played in her recovery. Danielle said, "It's I think the only reason that I am at the level that I'm at right now. My husband would come in the morning to the hospital and tell me, 'The whole world is praying for you. I'm getting messages from Italy, from France…' and then I didn't feel like I was doing it on my own anymore…knowing that everyone was reaching out to God and praying to move (my recovery) forward meant that I could just rest in knowing that. That's what being a community is.

Those prayers are what motivated me to go through those scary moments."

One of the most remarkable things that occurred during this time, circles back to the candles. Danielle said, "Denny and my mom and family would explain to me that people are lighting candles across the world. I'd close my eyes and I could see that, like flickering flashes of light – like a candle." She said that it was comforting and encouraging to feel that presence. What a remarkable manifestation of the power of prayer!

There's something else that we can all benefit from in exploring Danielle's faith, and that's in the intensity and confidence of her prayer. She said that she knew God was listening. From her own description, it sounds like she prayed to God with the same level of international record-breaking determination that she had employed so many other times in her life. She repeated these prayers, saying to God, "Failure is not an option for either one of us. I'm going to tell you what success is going to look like."

If that's not an example of confident prayer, I don't know what is! As our conversation drew to a close, Danielle shared a particularly relevant and poignant perspective on doubt within the context of faith. "Having faith and believing in God doesn't mean that you never have doubts," said Danielle, "A lot of people will move away from (faith), because they become discouraged by their own doubt."

It's a different take on the role of doubt in one's spirituality. She feels that it can be a positive thing. Danielle said, "I think those doubts are what give you the opportunity to build that relationship even more."

Ultimately, what she's saying is that having questions or being skeptical should not be a deal breaker. A lot of people walk or even run from religion or from their relationship with God, simply because they have doubt. Danielle's perspective is that it's more important to figure out what one's faith means to them and how they can best connect in their own way.

She's right about this. In fact, people who routinely avoid relationships or commitments because they have some doubt often live very lonely and unfulfilled lives. Everyone has some level of doubt when it comes to their spirituality, but that doesn't mean we should toss it out entirely. Perhaps it's just easier to reject the whole idea of faith, rather than putting some work into it. As mentioned earlier in this chapter, faith is not easy; it takes work. But as we can learn from Danielle's miraculous recovery, it's very well worth the effort.

Danielle's healing in the face of an extremely unlikely recovery is just one of so many examples that effectively illustrate the power of prayer. Her courageous life story also exemplifies the concept of resilience, a vital human quality that was the focus of Chapter 7 in this book. Danielle's life is one of remarkable faith and determination. Her story reinforces the importance of prayer in healing and provides a very positive note to savor; that of **hope**.

Ultimately, when people are in serious emergency or dire situations and need healing or rescue, they or their loved ones almost always ask for the same thing. The phrase, "thoughts and prayers" is the customary request when communicating with friends, colleagues or even to an entire community during a media interview. The more serious the circumstance, the more likely the word *thoughts* is no longer part of the request; instead, *prayer* becomes the sole appeal. Why is it that, regardless of religious affiliation or depth of spirituality, we humans somehow intrinsically know that prayer is the most important thing that we can rely on when times get really tough and we feel powerless?

Ask anyone if they believe in God, what they think about the concept of heaven or an afterlife, or about their view of divine intervention. Whatever they may say may not be at all reflective of how they feel about these concepts when they or their loved ones face mortality or a struggle that can't be overcome in conventional ways. At these times, even for lifelong disbelievers, somehow, the belief in the power of prayer and in the divine provides much comfort and hope.

In the end, whether you believe that prayer and spirituality have a tangible positive impact on healing or you doubt that such a relationship exists, it would be very difficult, if not impossible, to convince someone who has been the beneficiary of prayer-based healing, that it is folly. In as much as the relationship has been proven in hundreds of peer-reviewed studies, it would be worthwhile to at least have an open mind and give it a try. Unlike a lot of things in life, prayer is free.

This brings us full-circle to one of the questions near the beginning of this Chapter; "**Who are you in the universe?**" Your answer to that question may have been influenced by the pandemic. Are you as hopeful today as you were before the pandemic started? Has it made you re-think things that you previously took for granted, such as how fragile our world and our freedoms are? You see, you may not have changed at all physically or even emotionally in any significant way, but your concept of the world and your place in it may have changed subtly.

If, upon deep reflection, you now realize that the world seems more fragile than it seemed before, that our circumstances are not as clear-cut and predictable as you once thought they were, and that, perhaps you're not quite as hopeful about the future as you previously were, then my friend, your thinking – your perspective – has changed. It may be an optimal time to invite God into your life or if you already have but have neglected the relationship, to re-ignite that relationship.

I can't predict or guarantee much about things in my own life, let alone yours, but I am fairly confident that by nurturing a strong relationship with God and focusing on spirituality, those shaky new perspectives just mentioned will no longer bother you. I know it sounds cliché, but with God as your co-pilot, the awareness that circumstances are not as predictable is not nearly as troubling. In a similar way, with God, diminished hope becomes enhanced hope. This renewed perspective feels a lot better than the former alternatives!

As we welcome God into our lives and accept that He does have a plan for us, it becomes easier to understand and believe that He did use his love and divine power to create each one of us as a unique and sacred being! Remember that God does not make mistakes. So, who are you and how do you fit into the universe? There is only one of you in the entire universe and that's a pretty special thing, isn't it? Are you going to let the worries of the world consume and dictate what you do with your time in this universe or will you accept God's love and, in-turn, give love to others and accept it from them?

A good portion of this book relates to aspects of anxiety within the realm of the pandemic. Fear is one of the elements of anxiety. One thing that can help restore normality in your life is to choose to become more spiritual and to work on your relationship with God. God is bigger than any challenge you will ever face and He certainly doesn't want us to live in fear! By accepting God's love, fear dissolves.

How does one go about inviting God into one's life? One of the simplest things that anyone can do is to merely make an effort to acknowledge Him every day. In order to understand this concept, try seeing God as a part of your life from the very beginning. When you acknowledge this, a door opens. I can't describe the feeling of taking this first step on the journey to build your relationship with God, other than to describe it as beautiful.

In terms of strengthening one's relationship with God, there are countless ways in which an individual can nurture it. Starting each morning with prayer, reflection or just a casual conversation with God before we get out of bed is one way.

Living your relationship is another way. Practicing goodness, fairness, love and respect in your dealings with others reflects God's presence in your own life and extends it to others. Making sacrifices for others' good and even simple ways of making a positive impact on others further cements your relationship. Being optimistic, even when it's difficult, and expressing gratitude are practices that inspire others and so it gets passed along, like a set of tumbling dominoes. Finally, making God part of your personal and family traditions and rituals, such as attending church or worship, will also bring God closer to you and you closer to Him.

    The first few sentences in the Forward section of this book discuss how objectionable the phrase, *The New Normal* is; insofar as how people were predicting that the world would never return to normal after the pandemic. Perhaps that dismissal was a bit over-reaching; it may have had a more lasting negative effect than we wanted. But it could have a lasting impact in the opposite direction. Wouldn't it be great if one way in which the world changes through this pandemic is a new normal where our personal and global relationship with God is renewed and prioritized?

Stephen J. Kristof

Chapter 11
Believe in Good

Would it be reasonable to classify Covid-19 as an evil virus? Scientifically speaking, it's not a valid classification. Research virologists, biomedical engineers and biophysicists would describe the composition of this particular Coronavirus, Covid-19, as having 29,811 nucleotides, with coding for a total of 29 different viral proteins. At the same time, ask any ICU doctor or nurse who has tirelessly treated Covid patients over the term of this illness and it's unlikely that they would disagree with the statement that the virus is, indeed, evil. Someone who contracted the disease and fought their way out of an ICU or a family member of a loved one who died from it would most likely also agree that it is evil.

It would be difficult, if not impossible, to prove that the virus has evil intent; however, its aggressive method of transmission using human hosts makes it appear to have the intent to replicate. Regrettably, that replication can take the life of its human host. Whether the pathogen developed in nature through bats, pangolins or snakes, or was engineered and accidentally released from a research lab remains to be proven; perhaps we will never know where it came from. Nonetheless, regardless of how it came to be, or, whether or not it has intent, one thing is clear; **this virus has had a devastating impact on our world and for that reason, it is an evil presence in our world. Covid-19 has treated humanity with malevolence.**

The ravages of this pandemic shook our confidence and impacted our way of thinking in different ways. One way in which it left a lasting negative impression was in hiding the good that's all around us, while reinforcing and revealing the opposite of good. An interesting thing about human nature is our propensity, at times, to be attracted to things that aren't necessarily good for us. Perhaps it's less about human nature, but rather, our vulnerability to negative influences. Negative influences are, unfortunately, all around us; in our lives and in our world, but that doesn't mean we have to welcome them with open arms.

Regrettably, the pandemic was like a dark blanket of negativity that suffocated the world, quickly covering its far reaches. Pessimism and negative influence took root in a matter of mere weeks. It efficiently dulled humanity's collective feelings of hope, optimism and harmony, and instead, established a culture of fear, anxiety, dread, pessimism, discourtesy and distrust. As discussed earlier in this book, the media had some responsibility in propagating negativity, but so did we. It's not that we wanted to stamp-out hope and make things worse. It's just that, in conversation, we tend to be drawn to subjects that are more exciting and provocative; even if they are quite dreadful.

When meeting or talking with a friend, what are the usual topics of conversation? Most likely, you talk about things like news, sports, politics or personal things. Now, let's say that something has happened in your life that's really thrilling; maybe something that you've waited for a long time to happen. Perhaps it's a new car, a promotion at work, buying a nicer home, a big achievement, winning a competition – you choose. Like anyone, there's other stuff going on in your life, some good and some not-so-good things. There are also some pretty awful things happening in your city and in the world, be they political, health or environmental in nature. In this scenario, what are you most likely going to focus on in your conversation? That's an easy choice; if you're like most people, of course, you're going to talk about your personal good news! When something really positive is happening in our own little world, we naturally want to share that good news, whether to brag a bit or just to let others know how excited we feel.

However, in the absence of exciting and positive news about ourselves, the first choice of topic in this same scenario would naturally be the negative stuff that's occurring in our city, country or world. It's not that we want things to get worse, it's just that sensational information is more interesting. Anyone with a decent sense of social awareness realizes that their conversation partner really doesn't want to be stuck in an exasperating stream of the boring minutiae of life! As a result, most of us learn early in life to tailor our conversation to the most interesting topics which, unfortunately, are also very often negative topics.

There's no question that conversation in general during the past few years of this pandemic has been far more negative on average than before it started. However, we *can* take the reins and steer things in a better direction. **In the negative culture in which we are living at the moment, negativity only breeds more negativity. This is an exceptionally important concept to remember and to act on!**

Covid-19 may have planted the seed of negativity, but we need to stop fertilizing it. As humans, we have a responsibility to take a scythe to that malicious plant and cut it out by the roots. The truth is that our focus becomes our reality. One who is mired in pessimism about the world and angry about what's wrong in one's life most often gets more negative outcomes. It's not a coincidence! We can literally make things worse by focusing on what we don't have and on how unhappy we are. Negative energy looks for a place to go and it's most comfortable in negative environments. When we dwell on the negative, our spirit becomes negative and sick; this is attractive to negative energy. Positive energy is not comfortable where it's not welcome! In essence, by thinking, talking and behaving in a way that is pessimistic, uncaring, ungrateful and fearful, we open the door to more of it and close the door to positive things.

If you're a baby boomer or are even more 'mature' than that, you likely remember the iconic cartoon character, "Joe Btfsplk". Joe who? Seriously, you probably know the character, but just don't remember his name. He was the guy in the Li'l Abner newspaper cartoon series by Al Capp, who had a perpetual dark storm cloud hovering over his head. Now do you remember? Even if you don't recall him, Joe was an important character, because he symbolized the idea that negative begets negative. It wasn't that Joe was jinxed; rather, he jinxed everything that could have been good by believing that only bad things would come his way. He was correct.

The good news is that the opposite is also true! The more we reinforce positivity in our life through affirming self-talk, optimistic conversation with others, appreciative meditation and thankful prayer, the more we increase the likelihood of positive things happening in our life. Living in gratitude and reflecting on our blessings, such as our opportunities, our family, our material things, our job, our home, our health and other gifts, attracts even more positive things. Positive energy rests with the positive. Positive energy is most comfortable where it is welcome!

As difficult as the pandemic has been in different ways for each of us, it's imperative that we accept it and choose to move forward with positivity. Consider that, as much as we can attract energy into our personal life that is similar to our thought process, so too, can this occur on a global community level. Our world is sick right now; not merely from Covid-19 and its mutations, but also from tremendous self-perpetuated negativity. When large groups of people share a similar culture of mood, the group invites and engages energy corresponding to that same mood.

To be realistic, it's unlikely that, as a global community, we can merely think the pandemic away. On the other hand, we can extend the suffering, the length of time it's in control and other parallel ills (such as division among people and nations), by attracting negative energy. You can't do it by yourself, but you and I and everyone else on this planet are an important part of the global community. Your personal commitment to positive thinking and, thereby, attracting positive energy is integral to a global effort. In other words, don't discount your own role in this. **The key is to create a culture of hope.**

The fact is that even during the height of the pandemic, even as the dark clouds gathered, we were surrounded by more good than bad and more hope than dismay! It was just hard to see, because of all of the negative reinforcement. Maybe that was an integral part of a malevolent virus. Not only did it kill, infect with illness and bring the world to a halt; it also infected us with doubt and gloom.

Creating a culture of hope will take a commitment to make a conscious and enthusiastic effort to focus on the positive:

Remain positive in your private thoughts, in your words to others and in your spiritual connection or prayer. Strengthen your spirituality through prayer and meditation;

Actively look for and acknowledge the good. In terms of the pandemic itself, look for ways in which you have personally grown through the challenge;

Ignore the sensational gloom and doom in the news – we've all heard it and, frankly, nobody wants to hear it anymore;

Despite the brooding and often upsetting media reports, look for and focus on the glimmers of hope regarding progress we've made in winning this battle;

Be grateful for your own blessings and for those of your loved ones and friends;

Stop participating in or spreading gossip that cuts down others; doing so is cowardly and hurtful, and it aggressively attracts negative energy into your own life;

Drop vengeance and the blame game – be compassionate and forgiving instead;

Reject negative energy in the form of hateful falsehoods that are meant to separate people, and outlandish conspiracy theories that erode common sense and human intelligence;

Seek out opportunities to share and celebrate love, creativity and the beauty of our world.

Ultimately, we have lived through one of those awful events that seem to come along every hundred years or so. As we continue to work together as a global community to eradicate the virus and its threat, it remains our choice as to whether or not we remain hopeful.

Always remember that light consumes darkness. The virus is not in charge and whatever havoc it may have wrought in your own life is part of the past. Look ahead and illuminate your path forward with the positivity of light and hope.

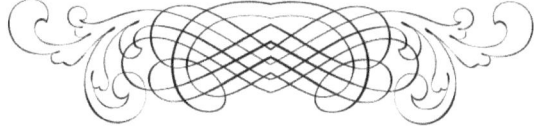

Stephen J. Kristof

End Notes:

[i] United States, Office of the President. "Press Briefing by President Joseph R. Biden." *The White House, Remarks by President Biden on Passage of the Bipartisan Infrastructure Deal*, Nov. 6, 2021.
https://www.whitehouse.gov/briefing-room/speeches-remarks/2021/11/06/remarks-by-president-biden-on-passage-of-the-bipartisan-infrastructure-deal/

[ii] Wee, Sui-Lee, and Vivian Wang. "China Grapples with Mystery Pneumonia-like Illness." *The New York Times*, 6 Jan. 2020, www.nytimes.com/2020/01/06/world/asia/china-SARS-pneumonialike.html

[iii] *Can the "new normal" ever go back to the old one?* (n.d.). Www.cbsnews.com. Retrieved October 10, 2021, from https://www.cbsnews.com/news/can-the-new-normal-ever-go-back-to-the-old-one/ ; *Story produced by* Mary Raffalli and edited by George Pozdere

[iv] *US & Allied Killed and Wounded | Costs of War*. (2018). Brown.edu. https://watson.brown.edu/costsofwar/costs/human/military

[v] Brink, Susan. "Can't Help Falling in Love with a Vaccine: How Polio Campaign Beat Vaccine Hesitancy." *NPR*, NPR, 3 May 2021, https://www.npr.org/sections/health-shots/2021/05/03/988756973/cant-help-falling-in-love-with-a-vaccine-how-polio-campaign-beat-vaccine-hesitan

[vi] Galbraith, Alex. "Florida Gov. Ron DeSantis Calls Record Covid-19 Numbers a Media-Fueled 'Hysteria'." *Orlando Weekly*, Orlando Weekly, 18 Aug. 2021, https://www.orlandoweekly.com/Blogs/archives/2021/08/03/florida-gov-ron-desantis-calls-record-covid-19-numbers-a-media-fueled-hysteria

[vii] Alvim, Leda. "Florida's Covid-19 Deaths Are Still among the Highest in the Nation." *WUSF Public Media*, 15 Oct. 2021, https://wusfnews.wusf.usf.edu/health-news-florida/2021-10-14/floridas-covid-19-deaths-still-among-the-highest-in-the-nation

[viii] Schive, Kim. "Breakthrough Infections: What You Need to Know." *MIT Medical*, 5 Apr. 2021, medical.mit.edu/covid-19-updates/2021/08/breakthrough-infections

[ix] Gamillo, Elizabeth. "Unvaccinated Individuals Are 11 Times More Likely to Die From Covid-19." *Smithsonian Magazine*, 20 Sept. 2021, www.smithsonianmag.com/smart-news/unvaccinated-individuals-are-11-times-more-likely-to-die-from-covid-19-than-those-who-are-vaccinated-180978714

[x] Disasterphilanthropy.org, 2021, https://disasterphilanthropy.org/disaster/2019-ncov-coronavirus/?gclid=CjwKCAjw8KmLBhB8EiwAQbqNoLNE5nQa8lgrh-_lSRwasVuQLF61_LXskgAD4bUwhpkffYMh9OUmSxoC9ooQAvD_BwE

[xi] Udalova, Victoria. "Initial Impact of COVID-19 on U.S. Economy More Widespread than on Mortality." *The United States Census Bureau*, 8 Mar. 2021, www.census.gov/library/stories/2021/03/initial-impact-covid-19-on-united-states-economy-more-widespread-than-on-mortality.html

[xii] Padhan, Rakesh, and K.P. Prabheesh. "The Economics of COVID-19 Pandemic: A Survey." *Economic Analysis and Policy*, Feb. 2021, 10.1016/j.eap.2021.02.012.

[xiii] "USAspending.gov." www.usaspending.gov, www.usaspending.gov/disaster/covid-19?publicLaw=all

[xiv] Doghramji, MD, Karl. "The Epidemiology and Diagnosis of Insomnia." *The American Journal of Managed Care*, May 2006, https://media.mycme.com/documents/20/doghramji_2006_4855.pdf

[xv] "PTSD from COVID-19? What You Should Know." *Cedars-Sinai*, www.cedars-sinai.org/blog/ptsd-covid-19.html.

[xvi] Spiegel, David. "85% of American Workers Are Happy with Their Jobs, National Survey Shows." *CNBC*, CNBC, 2 Apr. 2019, www.cnbc.com/2019/04/01/85percent-of-us-workers-are-happy-with-their-jobs-national-survey-shows.html

[xvii] Rudroff, Thorsten et al. "Post-COVID-19 Fatigue: Potential Contributing Factors." *Brain sciences* vol. 10,12 1012. 19 Dec. 2020, doi:10.3390/brainsci10121012

[xviii] Malone, Kelly Geraldine. "Parents Concerned about COVID-19 in Schools, 8 in 10 Support Mask Mandates: Survey." *Global News*, 13 Oct. 2021, https://globalnews.ca/news/8259238/parents-covid-19-schools-majority-support-mask-mandates-survey

[xix] Shamus, Kristen Jordan. "Flu Rips through University of Michigan Campus, Bringing CDC to Ann Arbor." *Detroit Free Press*, Detroit Free Press, 15 Nov. 2021, www.freep.com/story/news/health/2021/11/15/flu-rips-through-university-michigan-campus-brings-cdc-campus/8622063002/

[xx] "Covid: Austria Introduces Lockdown for Unvaccinated." *BBC News*, BBC, 15 Nov. 2021, www.bbc.com/news/world-europe-59283128

[xxi] "Insomnia: How Do I Stay Asleep?" *Mayo Clinic*, 23 Aug. 2019, www.mayoclinic.org/diseases-conditions/insomnia/expert-answers/insomnia/faq 20057824

[xxii] "New Survey Reveals Post-Pandemic Work Attire: 'Everyday Feels like Casual Friday.'" *Businesswire.Com*, 27 Oct. 2021, https://www.businesswire.com/news/home/20211027005272/en/

[xxiii] Kemp, Simon. "Digital 2020: Global Digital Overview." *Datareportal.Com*, DataReportal – Global Digital Insights, 30 Jan. 2020, https://datareportal.com/reports/digital-2020-global-digital-overview

[xxiv] Jordan, Alexander H., and Brett T. Litz. "Prolonged Grief Disorder - American Psychological Association." *American Psychological Association*, Professional Psychology; Research and Practice, 2014, https://www.apa.org/pubs/journals/features/pro-a0036836.pdf

[xxv] Brockmann, Hilke et al. "Time to retire--time to die? A prospective cohort study of the effects of early retirement on long-term survival." *Social science & medicine (1982)* vol. 69,2 (2009): 160-4. doi:10.1016/j.socscimed.2009.04.009

[xxvi] Marcus, Jon. "Pandemic Forced Millions of Workers to Retire Early." *AARP*, 10 Mar. 2021, https://www.aarp.org/work/working-at-50-plus/info-2021/pandemic-workers-early-retirement.html

[xxvii] Association: Dr. Chittaranjan Andrade (at the time of this writing) Dean and Professor of the Department of Psychopharmacology at the National Institute of Mental Health and Neurosciences, Bangalore, India

[xxviii] Association: Dr. Rajiv Radhakrishnan (at the time of this writing) Assistant Professor of Psychiatry at Yale School of Medicine

[xxix] Andrade, Chittaranjan, and Rajiv Radhakrishnan. "Prayer and healing: A medical and scientific perspective on randomized controlled trials." *Indian journal of psychiatry* vol. 51,4 (2009): 247-53. doi:10.4103/0019- 5545.58288

[xxx] Koenig, Harold G. "Religion, spirituality, and health: the research and clinical implications." *ISRN psychiatry* vol. 2012 278730. 16 Dec. 2012, doi:10.5402/2012/278730

[xxxi] Wilhelm, Trevor. "Miraculous Turnaround: Misdiagnosed with Muscular Dystrophy, Paralympic Star Campo Finds New Hope with Medical Breakthrough." *Windsorstar*, Windsor Star, 18 July 2020, http://windsorstar.com/news/local-news/miraculous-turnaround-misdiagnosed-with-muscular-dystrophy-paralympic-star-campo-finds-new-hope-with-medical-breakthrough

[xxxii] Maluske, Michelle. "'I'm Still Shocked That I'm Here': Windsor Paralympian Back at Home Five Weeks after Being on Life Support." *Windsor*, CTV News, 3 Nov. 2021, http://windsor.ctvnews.ca/i-m-still-shocked-that-i-m-here-windsor-paralympian-back-at-home-five-weeks-after-being-on-life-support-1.5650584

[xxxiii] Campo-McLeod, Danielle. Telephone interview with the Author. 22, Nov. 2021.

About the Author

Stephen Kristof is a Writer/Author who has built a strong foundation of diverse insights throughout his extensive career. He has held various capacities related to media, management, education, consulting and creative arts. Throughout this time, he has had the privilege to guide, counsel and educate people of all ages and from every walk of life.

His interesting career history spans several widely-varied roles, including teaching journalism and media studies, owning and operating a local advertising and public relations firm, managing a bustling career consulting company, serving as a supervisory employment consultant with a Fortune 500 company, voicing a weekly column on local radio, working for a national broadcaster, operating a popular photography skills website, and more.

Stephen's academic credentials include Degrees in both Communications and Education, along with various certifications and training. When he's not writing, he enjoys taking-on occasional voiceover talent jobs. For leisure, he loves to wear his photographer hat to create artistic images such as the one on the front of this book. When he puts down his camera, he's often up to his elbows in soil, as he is an avid gardener.

Beyond all of that busy and creative stuff, Stephen's most important priorities in life are his family and his spirituality. He loves nothing more than being a husband, father, son, brother, uncle, nephew and brother-in-law, while celebrating the gift of life and love with his family and friends.

Watch for Stephen's next book, a riveting and diverse collection of fictional short stories, to be released in 2023.

Visit **https://StephenKristof.com** for book giveaways, previews of his upcoming books and links to his video podcasts.
Stephen is available for speaking engagements and media interviews; contact him using the form on his website.

www.ingramcontent.com/pod-product-compliance
Lightning Source LLC
Chambersburg PA
CBHW072049110526
44590CB00018B/3093